From Wife to Widow

Dealing with Blood Cancer,
Grief and Life Beyond

Testimonials

"It covers the rollercoaster of life's emotions and for anyone who has been face down in heartbreak.

Suzanne's story is about bravely getting back up by owning her story, her actions and her need to heal, to find acceptance and to grow. Still experimenting, Still Learning, So Proud of You. Xx"
Nicola McCorley – Work Colleague and Friend

"The telling of Suzanne's story is authentic, entirely transparent and laced with the wisdom of one who has engaged the highs and lows of life. This is worthy of a 'must read' for those who find themselves experiencing a similar life journey or who have an interest in exploring the journey of loss and grief. I applaud Suzanne's courage in the telling of her story."
**Leanne Duncan – Chaplain,
The Wesley Hospital Brisbane**

"Suzanne's story is personal, intimate and shows vulnerability. I felt her love for Robert, her pain, and her loss through the pages. This story will make you remember what is important in life. The answer to what is the rainbow connection is Suzanne and Robert's everlasting love for each other."

Rebecca Warner – Friend

"'I cried myself to sleep.'

It's a phrase that we all might use if we were facing the loss of a cherished loved one or our eternal life partner to the scourge of cancer. But this amazingly written recount is far more than just a cliché or a tragic journey through the battlefield that is hospital wards, treatments and emotional struggles…it is a celebration of the indominable human spirit, of strength, fortitude and gratitude for the precious time we are blessed to spend with others."

Peter Hodson – Principal

"'Lover, I give you my hand! I give you my love, more precious than money, I give you myself before preaching or law: Will you give me yourself? Will you come travel with me? Shall we stick by each other as long as we live?' (Walt Whitman)

"When two people take each other "in sickness and in health" it is probably a good thing they cannot know the future. For every now and then these words are truly put to the test.

Suzanne and Robert had a happy marriage. Then, one day, their life changed.

"Robert goes to the medico and out of left field hears the sentence which, from that moment, changes his life and her life.

"Robert has leukaemia. The narrative of their life then becomes the day to day and year to year struggle to extricate happy living from a fearful and unpredictable disease.

"The book is very readable and engaging from beginning to end. It is written by a wife and soulmate who truly and passionately loves her husband and knows what the commitment of marriage really means. It is not only a clinical history of the illness itself but, more importantly, it is an emotional history - the feelings and fears with which the soul has to cope. The emotional quotient of the writer is in the Mensa scale and she savours every moment of worth from the time with her husband. I was amazed that anyone could remember the emotional and clinical details which frame this love story.

"I learned later the author had kept a journal which gave me, for some reason, a feeling of relief. The ups and downs of Robert's struggle would be obviously helpful to anyone battling with leukaemia or indeed any other serious disease.

"Those who love deeply will grieve deeply". This is also a story of grief, but it rests on a soft cloud of human connection from the natural family and the chosen family who surround Robert and Suzanne with love and support at every point in the Journey. Parents, relatives, long-standing friends, short-standing new friends, medical and social professionals - a community of compassion which never left them to tremble or weep alone."

Dally Messenger III – author, publisher, commentator, celebrant

First published by Ultimate World Publishing 2021
Copyright © 2021 Suzanne Gomes

ISBN

Paperback: 978-1-922497-48-2
Ebook: 978-1-922497-49-9

Suzanne Gomes has asserted her rights under the Copyright, Designs and Patents Act 1988 to be identified as the author of this work. The information in this book is based on the author's experiences and opinions. The publisher specifically disclaims responsibility for any adverse consequences which may result from use of the information contained herein. Permission to use information has been sought by the author. Any breaches will be rectified in further editions of the book.

All rights reserved. No part of this publication may be reproduced, stored in or introduced into a retrieval system, or transmitted in any form, or by any means (electronic, mechanical, photocopying, recording or otherwise) without the prior written permission of the author. Any person who does any unauthorised act in relation to this publication may be liable to criminal prosecution and civil claims for damages. Enquiries should be made through the publisher.

Cover design: Ultimate World Publishing
Layout and typesetting: Ultimate World Publishing
Editor: Isabelle Russell

Ultimate World Publishing
Diamond Creek,
Victoria Australia 3089
www.writeabook.com.au

In loving memory of Robert Brian Gomes.

You will always be my inspiration. The one that reminded me that "if you haven't tried it, you can't say you can't do it or don't like it".

You will be in my heart forever.

I will love you to eternity.

Contents

Testimonials	iii
Introduction	1
Chapter 1: Life before Leukaemia	5
Chapter 2: Our Nightmare Begins	9
Chapter 3: The Challenges of Chemotherapy	17
Chapter 4: Braving a Bone Marrow Transplant	31
Chapter 5: The Power of Social Media	47
Chapter 6: Life after Transplant	51
Chapter 7: Confronting Anxiety	61
Chapter 8: The Reality of Relapse	67
Chapter 9: Pressure and Pain	85
Chapter 10: The Dress Rehearsal	95
Chapter 11: The Rollercoaster Ride	109
Chapter 12: Hope Turns to Heartache	119
Chapter 13: Losing the Fight	125
Chapter 14: Till Death Do Us Part	137

Chapter 15: A Fitting Tribute	157
Chapter 16: Life Without Robert	167
Chapter 17: Bad Luck Comes in Threes	175
Chapter 18: The End of a Career	187
Chapter 19: A Year of Firsts	191
Chapter 20: Moving Forward	211
About the Author	215
Acknowledgements	217

Introduction

At 26, I became a wife. At 46, I became a widow. It has been 18 months since my husband died and I still do not refer to myself as a widow.

The woman I was before the 10th of June 2019 has gone, and slowly evolved into a new woman, a new person, with a new purpose and a new identity. On that day, I lost a large part of who I was. But as time has gone on, I have understood that I have had to leave that Suzanne in the past. Like a tree that sprouts after a bushfire, I will sprout with new ambitions, a new purpose, and a new outlook on life.

When I first started writing my story three years ago, I intended for it to be a story of hope, of renewing your life after blood cancer. In my case that is still the intention, but for my husband, that was not to be. After nearly six years of hospitals, chemotherapy, medications and many days of hope, my forever till eternity husband died.

Those days leading up to Robert's passing and after are days that I will never forget. Losing someone that you thought was your 'happy ever after' at the age of 47 just did not make sense. Why Robert, why me, why was he chosen to leave us so early?

After a year of asking why, I came to realise that all of Robert's dreams, his 'bucket list' had been ticked off. That his work on this earth had been completed. That his life had been perfected and now he was bound for bigger things that were not part of this world.

That was not the case for me. I started to realise that I had lost so many of my childhood goals and celebrations, that at this time of my life, may not ever happen again.

Before I tell you anymore about that day, I want to tell you my story. My story of how I dealt with being his carer. About being Robert's wife, his confidant, his best friend and sometimes his enemy. I want to tell you what I went through, what I saw through my own lens and how I continued to face many challenges pre and post Robert's death.

For those who are mentioned in this book, your perspective of what was happening during these times may be different from my own. You may think that what I have written was not what was going on for you. But this is what I saw, when I was grieving, while with Robert.

I am not telling this story to gain sympathy, but rather as therapy to mend my broken heart and understand my grief. In healing myself, I hope to help heal other widows and widowers who read my story and realise that what they are experiencing is normal.

My story is not just about hurt, sadness, exhaustion, confusion, anger, and everything else major trauma brings to a human being. It is also one of strength, courage, resilience, wellbeing, and change.

Introduction

It is about how I dealt with what was thrown at me. How life's challenges, become your learnings for your next path in life? How to get yourself up each day, do it all again and most importantly how to find some sort of happiness in your day to day life?

My story is because of my husband and it is about how it has influenced who I am becoming.

Chapter 1

Life before Leukaemia

My husband and I had been married for nearly 14 years before our world was turned upside down. From the moment we met, we shared so many similarities. We worked together at the same company, barracked for the same football team, and loved sport, adventure and travelling. So, it did not take long before our attraction turned into love and we took the first step to be together.

Our relationship was a whirlwind once we got together. Going on dates, meeting each other's friends, enjoying the happiest life and it only took Robert six months before we took off overseas and Robert proposed to me on top of the Eiffel Tower.

He got down on one knee in the freezing cold on the 21st of November 1998 and asked me to marry him. Of course, I said yes and could not wait to be Robert's wife.

We were married 12 months later on the 27th of November 1999 at a winery in Sunbury, Victoria. It was the perfect day; my childhood dream was fulfilled. We celebrated in style with our family and closest friends and honeymooned in Port Douglas. What a way to kick off our life together, and both of us could not have been any happier.

We bought and moved into our first home in February 2000 in Hoppers Crossing, Victoria. It was the perfect three-bedroom, two-bathroom home and had a picket fence with a rose garden. Our house was our home and had the fairy tale facade that I had pictured when I was a kid.

Every year we would travel overseas to places where we would have adventures and create amazing memories. From Africa to Asia, South America to Mexico, India to Egypt, to name just a few. There was always a new place to travel to and explore every year.

We both had a love of sport and would watch our beloved North Melbourne Kangaroos every week whether at the ground or on television. We also loved going and watching the cricket, tennis, motor sport and athletics. I had a love of ballet and Robert would take me to the ballet for my birthday every two years. We went to several concerts, stage shows and movies. We did so much together and we were always willing to try new things.

We also had a great group of family and friends that we created memorable times with, which always included lots of laughter. Our outlook on life was always positive and we enjoyed the simple things.

Our group of friends was diverse. Friendships from the neighbourhoods we grew up in, from school, work, holidays, and we were the couple that just got along with anyone. We were value led and just genuine, good people to be around. Although we loved being with people, we also loved living a life of our own. Just the two of us enjoying the love we had for each other.

So, when we made the decision to move from Melbourne to Brisbane in August 2009, it just seemed like the right next step in our life together. We had been married for nearly 10 years, I had a great opportunity with my employer and it was another adventure for both of us.

During the next four years in Brisbane our friendship group would continue to extend. We missed our family and friends in Melbourne, but we always knew they were only a phone call or two-hour flight away. It also gave them a place to visit, bring their kids and create more memorable times in a different city.

We had embedded ourselves into the slower pace of Brisbane, with the Sunshine Coast and Gold Coast on our doorsteps. We renovated our house in Brisbane, installed a pool, and enjoyed a lifestyle that was predominately outdoors.

Our first 15 years together were filled with happiness. Sometimes, I would pinch myself on how fortunate we were and it was all on the back of the love that we shared and the respect and trust we had in each other. Robert was my soulmate and I was his. I felt that nothing could ever tear us apart for the next 40 years.

We had a magical day as you can see from our smiles

Chapter 2

Our Nightmare Begins

In August 2013, Robert completed Tough Mudder, an 18-kilometre obstacle adventure course on the Sunshine Coast that supported ex-war victims with the proceeds from ticket sales. Robert gathered a group of friends of all ages and different backgrounds to participate and he was the captain.

The training regime in the build-up was quite intense, and I had been training with Robert in the gym. Two weeks before the event, Robert had a bout of influenza and had to taper down his training and I remember running faster and longer then him during one training session. At the time I saw this as a win, rather than questioning what was going on with Robert's health.

On the day of Tough Mudder, Robert completed the course with the assistance of his six friends and an asthma pump. I was so proud that Robert had completed the event, he had captained his team and displayed such resilience whilst dealing with influenza.

In the coming weeks, Robert's symptoms became worse and was not able to shake the influenza symptoms. He started to get night sweats, he was not eating as much and was very fatigued.

After three weeks of not being able to shake his symptoms, after having a bin full of empty cold and flu packs I asked Robert to make an appointment with our doctor. In the last four years that we had lived in Brisbane Robert had not needed to see a GP. Even when we lived in Melbourne Robert never got sick. The doctor looked him over, sent him for blood tests and said she would have the results back in a few days.

On the morning of Friday 13th of September 2013, I was in Bundaberg for a work commitment. When I came out of the meeting, I had eight missed calls from Robert. When I rang him back Robert told me that he had received a call from his doctor. The first question that the doctor had asked was, "Where are you?" Robert replied saying that he had just arrived at work after catching the bus there. She then asked, "How are you feeling?" Robert replied, "Ok, a bit tired, and I did have some trouble walking up the hill to the bus but I am just putting that down to the influenza."

The doctor then told Robert that he needed to get to emergency ASAP, asking, "Can someone take you, as your test results are telling us that your red blood counts are too low and it is a miracle you are still standing."

After being taken to the nearest hospital by a work colleague, Robert was greeted at the reception desk and told, "We have been waiting for you!" He was then taken straight into emergency, where he was

Our Nightmare Begins

hooked up to several machines and the doctors started treating him for pneumonia. After hearing this news, which I didn't expect, I drove back from Bundaberg immediately.

On my arrival, I could see Robert was pale, lethargic, and not looking well at all. The nurses had told us that Robert would at least be in hospital for the next few days to treat the pneumonia and that I should go home get some clothes for him as there were still more tests to be done.

At 6 p.m., Robert was taken away to have a bone marrow biopsy. Robert did not understand why he was having this procedure outside of having a haemoglobin reading (hb) of 62. Most adults have hb of 110-150. He did not ask any questions to why this was necessary and just went with the flow. As far as Robert was concerned, he had been diagnosed with pneumonia and this must just be another test that was relevant to that. But my gut was telling me something else and I always seemed to have good intuition.

Robert came back from the bone marrow biopsy a little worse for wear. It was a painful procedure on top of the pneumonia, and he wasn't up for much talking. After making sure he was ok, I went home had dinner and had a restful night's sleep.

On Saturday 14th of September, I received a call from Robert at around 11 a.m. asking me to come into the hospital immediately. He did not tell me anything else just that he needed to talk to me and wanted me there now. I could tell in his voice something was up so I immediately drove to the hospital which was only 15 minutes away.

When I arrived at Robert's room he was sitting on a chair facing the doorway and as soon as he saw me enter the room, he asked me to close the door and I knew something was not right. As I walked towards Robert, he burst into tears and all I heard him say was that he might have leukaemia.

I dropped to the floor in front of Robert, put my head in his lap and cried my eyes out with him. I can still hear those words, picture his face and remember the pain that I felt for my husband. How could this be, what did this mean. Three weeks ago, he was doing Tough Mudder, yesterday he had pneumonia, today he has leukaemia!

I started to ask Robert what he had been told but he could not remember too much and was in shock. He kept saying he might have leukaemia, but we should get the head nurse as he said he would explain everything to us when you arrive.

When the head nurse came, the story was a little different. They had confirmed with the haematologist that they did not think Robert might have leukaemia, he had leukaemia. My heart sank, my throat constricted and I felt like I could not swallow.

They then told us that Robert had an aggressive leukaemia called Acute Myeloid Leukaemia. It is usually diagnosed as a secondary leukaemia, although is generally diagnosed in men and the age group that typically get diagnosed as a primary leukaemia were a lot older than my 41-year-old husband.

We were told that Robert would start chemotherapy in the coming days, and that he would be in hospital for several weeks, and we were given a selection of reading materials that explained the diagnosis. The nurses were extremely helpful and after I asked several questions, they left us alone to discuss some of the decisions we needed to make quickly.

After more tears, I pulled myself together and started to contact our families in Melbourne. The phone calls seemed like they never ended, going over the same information. The call would start with, sorry for calling today, then I would begin to cry, and next it was, Robert is in hospital and has been diagnosed with leukaemia. On hearing the news our family and friends were in shock, they would break down and continually tell me that they could not believe it. Every call seemed to take at least 10 minutes, with them asking lots of questions that I could not answer.

It had been such a long and exhausting day, I felt like I had aged overnight. My eyes were red and stinging from all the crying, and I felt like my shoulders had bricks on them pushing me down. I kept looking at Robert and making sure he was ok, making sure he had everything that he needed but Robert was unusually quiet for most the night and exhausted as well. I could not imagine what was going through his head. For the first time ever, Robert and I were speechless and were not able to comprehend what the future held.

I remember the first night at home by myself after Robert's diagnosis. I read the books the nurses had given us on Acute Myeloid Leukaemia. I understood most of it and had written down some questions for the doctor when we were to meet with him on Monday. I then made a list of what I had to do over the following days and into the next week. There were so many more people that I had to ring, including both Robert and my manager from work.

That night was one of the worst sleeps of my life. I was sobbing in bed thinking of the worst. We did not know anyone who had had leukaemia, much less survived it, and I had so many questions circling in my mind. I kept saying to myself that Robert was going to survive, that he had more fight than anyone I knew and that he would be ok. But whilst I had the angels telling me everything was going to be ok, the devil in my mind was asking how was I going to live without Robert? What kind of funeral would Robert want? Do I stay in Brisbane after Robert dies, or do I move back to Melbourne? All of these questions kept running through my head all night.

After tossing and turning, at 2 a.m. I decided to get up and do some research via Dr Google. Through the search engine I typed in "people who have survived Acute Myeloid Leukaemia". Huge mistake, Suzanne. All I found were stories of people not surviving, enduring horrible side effects from their treatment and even patients calling out on the chat rooms asking people what they should do. The nurses had told me to only read the material they had given us and they would answer any questions I had. Instead, in my desperation to find an answer I wanted to hear, I had stupidly asked Dr Google, which was not helpful at all and all it did was close out my positive angels and bring back the devil. The devil that would tell me that my husband was destined to die and I had to start planning for the worst!

The next day, I arranged with my work to have a period of leave. We had been informed that Robert would have a minimum of four weeks in hospital, one week of chemotherapy, and three weeks of recovery. I also arranged for Robert to be off work indefinitely. We had been told that it would take two to three rounds of chemotherapy for Robert's bone marrow to respond and go into remission and if all went well, he would hopefully be on the road to recovery in January.

On Sunday when I arrived at the hospital, 24 hours after the diagnosis, Robert told me he was going to fight this disease. I was so overjoyed and emotional that I threw my arms around him, kissed him, and said I will fight with you too. Together we had survived charging elephants in Africa, conquered the altitudes of the Inca Trail, climbed Mt Fuji, and successfully completed caving in Belize. Robert just saw this as just another one of those challenges that would have a fairy tale ending and a story that we would tell our new and old friends for years to come.

Our Nightmare Begins

Throughout the days leading up to Robert starting chemotherapy, we had to make a few decisions and have some tough conversations. The first one was about whether we were going to have children.

Robert and I had tried to have a family a couple of times. We had been through all the tests when we could not conceive naturally. We considered IVF but never went through with it. We had always wanted to have children, but other priorities, work, our lifestyle, and holidays seemed to take top priority and now we had to decide in the next 24 hours on whether we really wanted to have a family.

Due to the effects the chemotherapy was going to have on Robert's body, the only way for us to conceive after this ordeal was over was for Robert to freeze his sperm now. The poor guy 24 hours earlier had been told he had a life-threatening disease, an aggressive blood cancer and now he had to think about the process of freezing his sperm. I told Robert that this was his decision, and if he didn't think he could go through with it, then I would support him.

I loved my husband so much. He is the most amazing man in the world and I did not want to put more pressure on him. After thinking about it for an hour and discussing what this would mean for us, Robert's decision was that he could not do it. He did not have the energy or maybe even the ability to donate his sperm and I accepted his decision whole-heartedly.

The second conversation was with the head nurse was about our marriage. They asked us about our relationship. Were there any issues related to our finances, children, family etc that had put pressure on our marriage. They also asked how we communicated, did we fight, did we work through challenges together.

Our relationship was always special, we were a couple that did not fight much at all. We maybe had a blow up every few years, and it was typically resolved within 24 hours. We did not have any financial issues, we had secure jobs and had open communication.

The head nurse really pressure-tested our responses until he was satisfied that there was nothing to uncover. He then told us the reason for all of his questioning. We were about to go through the biggest test of our marriage, our relationship. We were going to have to be both selfish and unselfish. Our ability to be free, loving individuals was about to be put on hold and we were told that if we had any issues before treatment, then the pressure of chemotherapy and long stints in hospital would be a pressure that we had never felt before.

I remember taking a step back, thinking it was ridiculous, as how could they know us after only being in the system for a few days. How would they think that this could possibly destroy our bond, our marriage? Unfortunately, these nurses had seen it all, the good times and the bad and everything in between. It is the nurse that discretely walks the halls, hears many conversations and emotions, and looks out for our welfare. So, if we did not admit to at least ourselves if there were any cracks in our relationship, it would be transparent soon.

Our world had now been turned upside down. We had gone from the fun-loving, social individuals into a system where we did not know how it would end and how we would cope. All our plans, our holidays, would now have to be cancelled for the next six months and we did not know whether Robert would survive the treatment. The only thing I knew was that Robert was a fighter, I was a fighter, and together we would hopefully win this fight and have a beautiful story to tell for years to come.

Chapter 3

The Challenges of Chemotherapy

On Monday 16th of September, we met Robert's haematologist. He said that they had got the disease relatively early and only 35 per cent of Robert's blood had leukaemia cells in it. He was young, fit, and healthy and had all the attributes to be able to survive this. He told us that he would give Robert introductory chemotherapy to start with, see how his body reacted to it and increase the dosage if all went well in round one.

On the 17th of September 2013, Robert received his first dose of chemotherapy. He was so upbeat, which created a great energy for me. The first round of induction chemotherapy was for seven days and Robert had minimal side effects. During that first week he would go down to the café and get a "real coffee". He had a daily routine of walking the ward ensuring he would not get any nasty blood clots that could hinder his recovery. He would go out onto the open-air courtyard in the ward every day and sit there for hours. The nurses worked out quite quickly that if they could not find Robert in his room, they could soon find him outside.

During the first round of chemo, I had friends come and stay with me at least a few days each week. They would visit Robert with me and when I came home, we would go out for dinner, debrief about the day and the company they gave me kept me positive. Since Robert was upbeat and fighting the good fight, then I was upbeat too.

There were moments through the first week, that were surreal. I could not believe the treatment was going so well. The doctor was happy with Robert's progress, they were forming a good doctor-patient relationship, and the ward was full of wonderful nurses. We felt that we had the best medical staff around us, which allowed us to feel we were in a supported and trusted environment.

On the second weekend Robert was having chemotherapy, three of my closest girlfriends came up from Melbourne. My first recollection of the weekend was walking into the house after visiting Robert on the night they arrived. I had left the keys for them so they were already in the house when I got home. There were lots of hugs, some tears and just a feeling of sadness. After a week in the hospital, I was beyond tears and just wanted to feel some sort of normality with my beautiful friends. These girls gave me an energy that I needed and a break from the eight to ten-hour days that I was putting in at the hospital.

Over the two days the girls were at our house, we had lots of laughs, plenty of wine, and many deep conversations. You should never push back the time a girlfriend or mate wants to spend with you during times like these. It is very therapeutic to have conversations that are not about blood cancer, chemotherapy, and hospitals. It is such a relief to go out to brunch, to enjoy good food and company, and it allowed me some time to focus on me and I did not feel guilty about it either.

During Robert's first round of chemotherapy, he only had a few visitors because he needed to be extremely careful. After the first seven days of chemotherapy Robert's immune system would drop down to zero and had no immune system to fight any infections. We had to ensure that anyone who visited had to be 100 per cent healthy so that he did not get sick. As part of this, I had to also make sure that I did not encounter anyone that was sick as I would not have been able to visit Robert daily. To be extra cautious I restricted my friends' visits for the three weeks Robert was immunosuppressed to just a handful of people.

Throughout Robert's treatment, his psychological wellbeing would be what would concern me the most. I found that when Robert entered his immunosuppressive state (he had no immune system which caused lethargy and fevers) he was very withdrawn. He would not come out of his room in fear of catching something and did not speak much. For a guy who had so many friends, who could possibly distract him from what was going through his head, it was jarring for me to see him push his friends away at this time. I never asked him why, but he just wanted to go through this with me and me alone.

The second week started to become tough, with fevers that we had both never experienced before. Robert would start to go pale, get cold and start to shiver. The rigours, which is what the nurses call them, would come on so quickly and when they came on, it was guaranteed that Robert's temperature would be above 39 degrees. I would get him a warm blanket maybe two, wrap them over him and talk to him while the nurses would administer Panadol which would reduce the temperature within 15 minutes. But those 15 minutes were so scary to watch. So, I had to keep calm, reassure Robert that everything was going to be ok, until the rigours disappeared. Every time I left the hospital after these fevers, I would cry all the way home. I felt so helpless and exhausted after the twelve-hour days, just wishing that I could take Robert's pain away.

During that week, my best friend Meagan visited. She is the most amazing, beautiful, and caring person in my world. Meagan and I have been friends since we were three. We lived next door to each other and although we did not go to school together, we did everything else together. From playing Barbies to me cutting Meagan's hair. To having our first cigarettes to going missing for hours on end. There was not much we did not do together when we were kids. In our adult years, Robert and I would visit her and Shane frequently. When Meagan had two girls, we became their godparents. Meagan was the sister I did not have.

When we visited Robert, we would not speak too much as Robert was in the immunosuppression stage, and he was quiet most of the time. Although when we left the hospital Meagan would listen to me pour my heart out on everything that had not been said that we had both witnessed. This part was hard for me, as I was still dealing with the prospect of what this meant to Robert and to me. I am usually a person that speaks three times the amount of words an average person would speak each day. But in this environment, silence and stillness was our new daily routine and I had to get accustomed to silence quickly.

During the second and third weeks of Robert's treatment, and especially when Meagan was there, whenever I seemed to do something for Robert, I just did not do it right which caused Robert to react negatively and get quite frustrated. Thankfully, Meagan talked me through this and told me that this is not the man I had married. His reactions and moods were completely driven by the treatment, the drugs and his inability to function outside the four walls of his room.

The Challenges of Chemotherapy

Watching my husband become a person that I did not recognise, that was not who I fell in love with, was hard. Sitting there most days with Robert for hours on end was never an effort for me, and I never regretted going home and having dinner late, sleeping in my bed by myself and doing it all again the next day. What I did have to focus on everyday was my love that I had for husband had not changed. It was still the same as the day that I had married him and this situation will not be here forever. By rationalising that every day it enabled me to get up and do it all again tomorrow.

By week four Robert's immune system started to come back to life. His demeanour started to change, he was eating more, talking more and now we had the next challenge of keeping him in until the doctor said he was right to go home. To ensure Robert and I were able to become accustomed to him being home and allow the extra days in hospital to pass by quickly, Robert was able to have a couple of hours leave pass from the hospital. The leave pass enabled us to either go home or go for a drive and return to the hospital at a certain time. Those days gave Robert so much energy and we would typically go down to the bay, get a coffee or some fish and chips and enjoy the warmth of the sun or the breeze from the sea. Sitting in the car in silence was a treat, and we took in all the positive energy that it gave us.

In preparation for Robert coming home, I was told that I had to have the house spotless. I had to wipe the benches down after every meal, have hand sanitiser on hand and make sure we washed the vegetables and fruit before eating them. This was to ensure that Robert did not pick up any nasty bugs that caused a secondary infection. So, the house was always spotless and I would ensure that I washed his clothes and towels after every use. Robert ended up being in hospital for 32 days for the first round of chemotherapy and it had been one of the longest months of both of our lives.

On the first night home, Robert had dropped quite a bit of weight over the first stint in hospital and his muscles had wasted away. To climb the 20 stairs into our house he needed help and he was puffing by the time he got to the top. He could not believe how the treatment had affected his stamina and that this was going to take some getting used to.

When I went to bed with him on that first night, I was lying next to him and it was so amazing to feel the warmth of his body next to me. In the middle of the night I awoke and I could not hear Robert breathing. There were no sounds outside, no sounds inside and I did not know if Robert was alive. I moved closer to him, still nothing, I put my hand close to his mouth, I could not feel a breath, I even tried to put my hand on his chest, nothing at all. I then called out softly, Robert, Robert and then shook him.

He jumped up so quickly, calling out what is it, what is wrong? I then jumped up myself and started to cry. I seriously thought Robert was dead. I thought he had died right next to me, but he was sleeping silently. At that moment before I fell back to sleep and as Robert hugged me I thought to myself, I never wanted to lose this warmth, I never wanted to lose his embrace, I never wanted to lose Robert.

When it was time for Robert to start round two, I had the support of my parents. They came up to Brisbane from Melbourne to care for me, whilst I went back to work. I would work from 7 a.m. to 3 p.m. every day, then visit Robert till around 7:30 p.m. before going home to a home cooked meal with my parents.

My mum and dad were so fantastic. They would do my washing, Robert's washing, the lawns, the gardens, any errands we needed done, and they basically became my full-time carers whilst I was Robert's. It made rounds two and three of Robert's chemo so much more bearable for me. It made me realise that I had two wonderful role models, loving individuals that would do anything to make this work for me and ensure they were by my side through this challenging time.

When I got home from the hospital we would talk about the day's events, other times we would watch television that took all of us to another world that did not involve blood cancer or hospitals. Anything to take the reality of the situation away for a few hours to allow me to recoup psychologically before going to bed.

But while everything seemed rosy to most people outside of my world, the pressure would get to me during round two. I had gone back to work three weeks into Robert's diagnosis and I was going through a major structural change which I was announcing to my team. My tolerance for egotistic individuals that believed I owed them was something I just could not tolerate. It was also at a time when I started to feel that some friends that were there for Robert were not there for me. But that is what happens when a loved one is sick, is affected by a disease like blood cancer. Most people care and put time in for the patient, and sometimes forget about the carer and although I was getting lots of love from my parents, when I was not getting the love that I needed from everyone it felt like they did not care.

One day at work, the world crashed on me. The pressure was too great, and my brain was in overdrive. It felt like everyone was by Robert's side, but who was by Suzanne's? I was believing what my mind was telling me, the devil was in full swing and I was imploding on myself. I could not allow Robert to see that I was not coping and the only place that I had to go was home. I have never been so angry, sad, and selfish in my entire life. I just wanted to go out and scream at all the people that were not standing by me, but at the same time I felt so angry at myself for being so selfish. I was not the one dealing with blood cancer.

I could not understand why people react differently in these circumstances. That sometimes your good friends have their own problems going on in life and distance themselves from you. That maybe they are dealing with their own grief as they may have had someone go through this previously. I felt like the walls were falling in, that I could not cope with the responses from the people around me and it was literally falling apart. I couldn't breathe, I couldn't stop crying, I was yelling and shaking. It felt like I was having a psychotic episode.

Thankfully, I had my beautiful friends, John and Di, staying at my house who calmed me down and talked me off the cliff. By now I was exhausted. The episode had taken so much out of me and I needed to sleep. The other thing I was grateful for was that my parents hadn't witnessed it. They were out of the house running errands and didn't see the extent of the breakdown and who I was angry with. John and Di were my saviours that day and they would go on to be my saviours many times over!

After this episode, it made me realise that I should have been talking more to my close friends, colleagues, and a professional on how I was feeling and dealing with Robert's situation. The impact that it was having on me was deeper than I had recognised and I had to admit that I didn't know how to deal with grief, anger, and especially blood cancer. At that point I didn't seek professional help. I just went through the motions of the day, made some changes emotionally on who I was going to depend on and made sure Robert did not know what had happened.

Robert went into remission after round two but as Acute Myeloid Leukaemia is an aggressive disease, he would need to have a further two rounds of chemotherapy and be in hospital for 28 days for each round to be sure they had killed all the bad cells.

The Challenges of Chemotherapy

It worked out that round three would take us up to Christmas, and, as most of us know, Christmas is a time you spend with your family, a time of cheer, where you are able to share the day with the people you love. My parents were going back to Melbourne to spend Christmas with my brother's family and their grandchildren. They deserved a break from the routine and we wanted them to have a happy Christmas without the sights of hospital.

So, we decided to have Christmas Day with our friends' parents. We refer to Ally and Daryll as our Queensland parents and they loved us as much as their son and daughter in law. We were so grateful to be able to spend it with people we loved although Christmas Day was bought with mixed emotions. We were thankful for Robert being with us, in remission and sharing the fortunes that life had given us, but I also felt different. I felt that something was not right. We were celebrating what, the end of the year, the end of a bad time in our lives, I just could not put my finger on it. The last three months had been the most emotionally driven months of my life. Balancing hospitals with work, balancing family emotions from miles away, putting my life on hold to ensure that my husband secured his.

By the end of the day and as we were leaving Ally and Daryll's it all got too much and I felt a wave of out pouring emotions when saying goodbye. It had not been the day I wanted, for me I had put on this brave face for Robert's sake. Every time I looked at Robert at the dining table, I saw a man that wasn't my husband. He was withdrawn, had no hair, he was thin and worn out. Looking at him made me sad even though Ally, Daryll and all the guests were doing their hardest to make it such a joyful day. I could not stop the tears as we left the house, I could not explain to my friends that it was not them it was me. In some ways although I was always putting on a strong, brave face, deep inside me I think I thought this may be the last Christmas with Robert. All I wanted that day was my husband by myself without the celebrations and just feel his warmth and touch.

New Year's Eve would come and go at the hospital. Robert had already started round four of his chemotherapy treatment and we watched the 8 p.m. city fireworks from the rooftop of the hospital with other families and patients that were going through similar treatments.

Standing together seeing the flashes of light in the sky gave me hope for a brighter and healthier 2014. That night I went home to an empty house. My family and friends would be celebrating bringing in the New Year with laughter and love. I would receive many drunken texts and phone calls calling out Happy New Year, and I would get off each call crying my eyes out. Before I went to bed, I said good riddance to 2013 and just hoped we would have a brighter 2014.

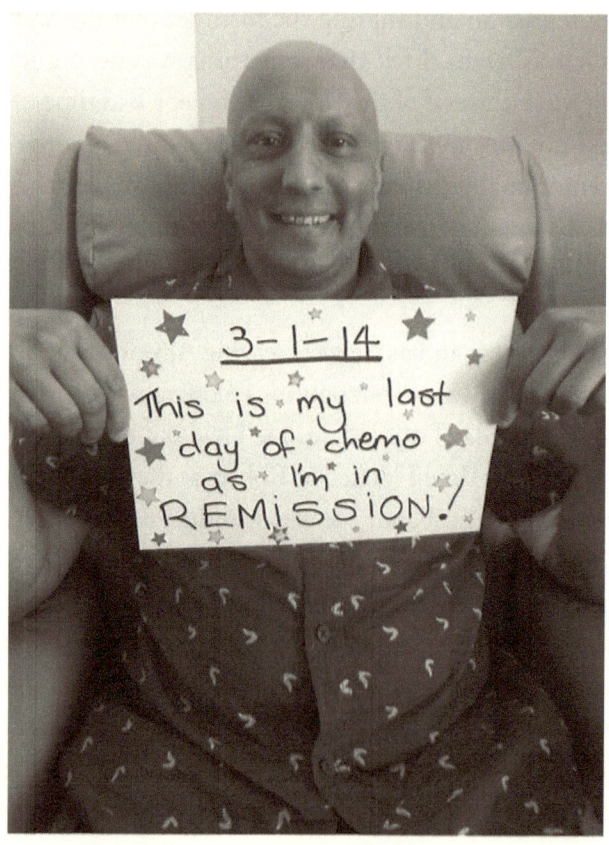

Round four started on a good note as Robert's body was used to the treatment and he was experiencing very few fevers. But halfway through January I received a call in the early hours of the morning saying that Robert had been taken to the Intensive Care Unit. He had contracted an infection that had affected his heart and the doctors had given him a shot of adrenaline as his heart rate had dropped below 40 beats per minute. The injection they had given would increase his heart rate although he was in a dangerous period. The ICU nurses told me not to come in yet, wait until 9 a.m. and they would call me if his situation deteriorated.

When I got the call that Robert was in ICU, I decided to do something that I had never done before: pray! I was not a religious person; I was christened Presbyterian but never practised religion. But that day, I felt I needed to introduce myself to whoever was looking down on us. If there was a God, and he could help, then this was the time I needed to call on him.

As I lay in bed, my words went along the lines of this:

"Hello, God, my name is Suzanne Gomes.

You don't know me, but I know you know my husband Robert Brian Gomes. He is currently in ICU and has leukaemia and today I thought I was going to lose him.

Now, I haven't always done the right things in life. I have committed a few sins, but my request today isn't for me, it is for my husband, and he needs your help, blessing. Whatever you do up there, he needs it. I have never asked anything from you, which is why I had to introduce myself. But, if you can hear me, then you know that my husband is the most generous, caring, loving individual and he needs your help tonight.

Thanks for listening and I hope I don't have to call on you again".

I remember laughing and crying at the same time after this. I was saying all of this out loud and for a moment I thought I was going crazy. But no, I was just doing what any loving person would do when someone needs a hand, even if it was way outside of my comfort zone for the man I loved!

With Robert now in ICU, I was doing 12-hour days at the hospital, holding his hand in the hope that he pulled through. He scared me a few times whilst in there, his heart rate and blood pressure dropped significantly a few times and nurses and doctors would rush to his bed side, make quick decisions, administer more drugs and within half an hour it was back to monitoring again. Thankfully, Robert is a fighter and he was able to pull through. He was determined this disease was not going to win and he stood up to the test and won this time.

On the 25th of January 2014, Robert was finally released from hospital and was in remission. It did not take long for Robert to regain his strength and he went back to full time work in March. We also had a remission party for Robert before he returned to work. Our house was full of family and friends from interstate and in Brisbane. The beautiful people that had stood by both of us during the last six months and we wanted to celebrate Robert's life and the people who loved us.

In the months following Robert's treatment, we gradually started to resume a normal life. We visited family and friends in Melbourne, started to attend weekly drinks with friends and I resumed my travel and commitments with work again.

In July 2014, to celebrate our return to a normal life, we took the opportunity to go on a once in a lifetime holiday to the Maldives. Robert had a work conference in Singapore and we decided to add on an extra ten days on an island, in an over the water bure, which was literally what the doctor ordered.

We relaxed, swam, wine and dined. I was so grateful that I had been given back the life that we had missed for six months. So grateful to be able to wake up every day, especially in the Maldives, in the arms of my wonderful husband and not have to worry about what the day held for him. It was like a second honeymoon and I know after what we had been through, we were so much more in love than ever before.

At home we had also returned to a fitness regime. We had a group of friends that we would do a 10-kilometre run/walk loop around the Brisbane River twice a week. Robert and I were going to the gym and we were preparing for two major events. In October, we were both doing a 5-kilometre fun run and I was doing a 60-kilometre walk over two days in Brisbane to raise money for the Queensland Institute of Medical Research. Both of us were feeling great and looking forward to achieving our fitness goals, and for me, raising vital cancer funds to enable further research to be undertaken on finding a cure for blood cancer.

Even though life had resumed to normal we continued to attend Robert's weekly, then fortnightly, appointments with his haematologist. I was not always in Brisbane for them but as we moved into October 2014, I felt that I did not have to and Robert would always pass on the information to me. We were living life to the fullest and we could not be happier. But what we did not know was that was all going to come to another big halt, and we would be thrown a curveball that would change our lives even more!

Chapter 4

Braving a Bone Marrow Transplant

In October, Robert's doctor asked that I attend the next appointment. He had not seen me for a while and said it was necessary. As we always did, we attended the Cancer Clinic and sat down across from the doctor. Robert would always start the conversation with some humour or banter, but today the doctor was serious and got straight to the point. Robert's blood results had changed, we were told that they had started to go in the wrong direction and he was heading towards relapsing.

The room fell silent and I remember saying what, what do you mean. I turned to Robert, he had tears in his eyes and then as we faced each other, tears fell onto our cheeks. I looked at the doctor and even he had tears in his eyes, his next words were, "I am so sorry, I didn't want to see this in your blood results either."

This must be the hardest part of any haematologists job. Having to tell patients that they had leukaemia or were relapsing. It was so hard to hear those words, but it must have been so hard for him to say them. But that word had been said, we heard it right: "relapse". Within a matter of seconds our thoughts turned from "how can this be?" to "what does that mean, what happens next?" The doctor proceeded to tell us that Robert needed a bone marrow biopsy today to confirm the diagnosis and a bone marrow transplant in the next month before he fully relapsed.

There are two types of bone marrow transplants blood cancer patients can have. A family match which is called Autologous, and a non-family match which is called an Allogeneic donor. A match has to be found via the patient's ethnicity. When Robert was first diagnosed and undertaking chemotherapy, his brother and sister were tested to see if they were a match, but unfortunately neither was. As Robert's parents are Anglo-Indian, we asked several of his cousins and uncles to be tested to see if they were a match, unfortunately none of them were either. So, between January and October, Robert's details had been loaded in the international bone marrow register and the search for a donor could happen behind the scenes.

On this day, the doctor told us that they had found an allogeneic match, an unrelated anonymous donor on the international bone marrow registry in another country. Bone Marrow Donors are exceedingly rare internationally. There are only 28 million people around the world on the registry, only 200,000 donors on the Australian Registry (sourced from the Australian Bone Marrow Donor Registry statistics), and not every country around the world has a register. Australia has several agreements in place with Donor countries to enable them to find donors for Australians. For Australians, you join the registry via your local Australian Red Cross Blood Donor Centre. You need to be between 18-45 and most Australians between these ages would meet the additional criteria's, but unfortunately knowing about going on this register is rare.

Part of the challenge in finding a donor for Robert was due to his ethnicity. Given that he was Anglo-Indian, the ability to find a donor was going to be tough. Luckily for Robert, they found a 30-year-old female donor, who we later found out lived in New York, who was willing to go through the procedure and hopefully save Robert's life.

Surviving the transplant was going to be an even tougher fight than the four rounds of chemotherapy that Robert had had. I never asked the doctor what the percentage mortality was. It was hard enough dealing with the thought of Robert having to go through this procedure much less what if he does not make it. But those thoughts come in and out of your mind on a semi regular basis and I just had to make sure that I did not attach myself to those thoughts. Robert had proven he could fight like Mohammed Ali and I knew he would bring his best fight to the ring.

Within a week of the news and confirmation that there were small amounts of leukaemia cells in Robert's bone marrow, Robert began six months sick leave from work. He had a list of things he wanted to get done and this would keep his mind busy.

On hearing the news his best mate came up from Melbourne and over five days they were able to complete a number of jobs around the house that Robert would not be able to do post his transplant. It was also a great time for James to be up with his best mate helping him out. James had been in total shock when he had heard the news of Robert's diagnosis twelve months ago. Unfortunately for James, his cousin had been diagnosed with Leukaemia when he was young and didn't win the fight. In some way spending this time with Robert was so precious to him and he was convinced that Robert had the strength to beat this disease.

On the 21st of November 2014 we drove to the Royal Brisbane Women's Hospital and stepped into ward 5C. We were introduced to the ward staff, allocated room 29, unpacked Robert's things and got settled in. We also met his next-door neighbour Rob! Yes, Robert and Rob were next door to each other. Rob was eight days ahead of Robert, had had his transplant that day and was in good spirits. It was nice to see someone in the ward that was ahead of Robert and we could see what was ahead of us. Plus, Rob had a fighting spirit like Robert so I knew from the start that they would be great mates by the end of this.

We had been relieved of hospitals for nearly ten months, and I seemed to have slipped back into the routine quite seamlessly. I had taken three months off work and my parents, without even asking had returned to Brisbane, to take up their role as carers for me. We took our allocated positions back in 'Team Gomes' and just started to do the tasks and support, that all three of us had done the previous year.

Seven days before Robert had the Bone Marrow Transplant, he had to have two doses of chemotherapy and six doses of full body radiation. The side effects of the treatment kicked in quickly. Robert had nausea and severe headaches. He was taking the strongest pain relief the doctors would administer, but the pain was so bad that he would hold his head or lie in the foetal position waiting for the next round of drugs and hope they would take effect quickly. He was in excruciating pain for those first six days and it was so hard to watch.

I learnt so much about the transplant process when talking to the nurses on the ward. Once a donor is selected and they say yes to being a donor, over a course of a week they have injections to increase the population of their stem cells. Basically, this means they have to create as many as they can in the donor's blood to be able to transfer them to the patient.

On the day of the retrieval of the cells, the donor will basically have a blood transfusion where they will take out the stem cells into a bag and transfuse the red blood back into the donor. At the time, I did not know a donor or what a donor has gone through but since then, my cousin's husband went on the register and has been a donor. He advised that it is non-evasive and simple compared to what the recipient goes through. He said he experienced some pain, but that pain would be overcome quickly on the knowledge that he was saving a person's life.

Something else I found out was if the donor is overseas a nurse, that works in the transplant ward, flies to the country to collect the cells. They will be there when the donor has the cell retrieval. They will then get on the plane with an esky that has the bag of cells in it. The cells then fly business class, they have their own seat and the nurse must ensure the temperature inside the esky is monitored throughout the flight. Sleep for the nurse is not really an option, and the flight attendants will keep additional cold packs cold so the nurse can swap them over during the flight.

When they arrive in the receiving country, they are transported to the transplant ward and stored in a fridge waiting to be transfused. For a nurse this is a serious responsibility and although flying to say Germany or America and back over three or four days may sound great, I was told it is an exhaustive process. But knowing they are potentially saving a life makes it all worthwhile.

On the 28th of November, two days after Robert's donor cells had been received from overseas, he had his transplant. Another amazing fact with the transplant process, is that if the blood type of the donor is different to the patient, within a few months the recipient's blood type will change. In Robert's instance he was O negative, but his donor was A positive, so his blood type changed to A positive. But what it also means is that when Robert's donor cells were transfused, he could have severe side effects as the blood types were different.

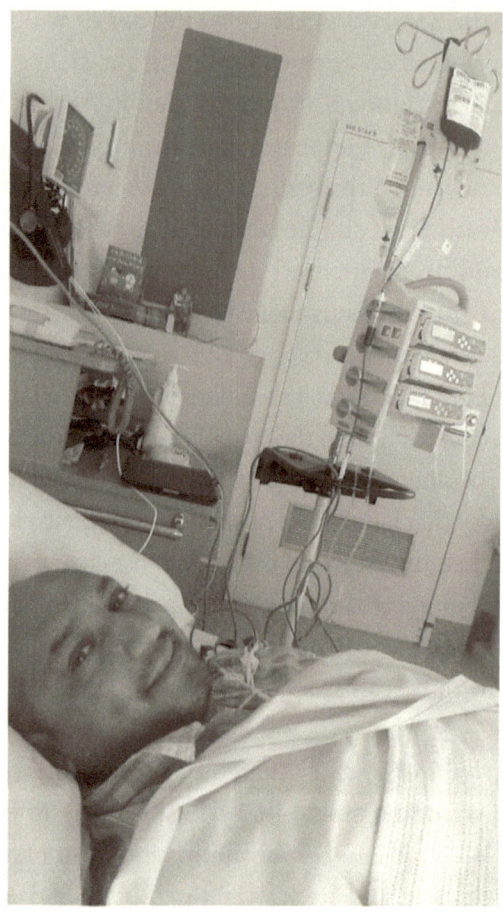

So, the cells were hung, the nurses had made a sign that they had stuck to the wall in Robert's room saying, "Happy Transplant Day", and then the transfusion begun. Robert slept through most of the transplant, as the lead-up had been quite exhausting. It only took an hour to transfuse the cells and as he got closer to the end of the transfusion Robert began shaking and had a fever due to the blood type difference. I remember watching the transfusion, mesmerised with every drop that was going through the line into Robert's body. The tears that feel onto my cheeks that day were tears of joy. The donor on the other side of the world, had unselfishly given the cells to save my husband's life. I didn't leave Robert's side through the whole process and was so grateful that he had the opportunity of a second chance in life.

A few days after the cells had been infused Robert's immune system dropped to zero and he started to have severe side effects. Over the next few days, Robert developed ulcers in his mouth to the point where it was too painful for him to eat anymore. The doctors started to feed Robert intravenously through his line and administered one of the highest pain drugs you can receive: ketamine.

Over the next two weeks Robert would be in an induced drug coma. He had no recollection of what occurred and, in some ways, I was thankful for that. But what he cannot remember has made an imprint in my mind to last a lifetime. Ketamine is a drug typically given to horses that are in pain. It is given intravenously 24/7 in a controlled dose. It allows the pain to be removed and makes the patient comfortable. Ketamine is also a street drug known as 'Special K'. Drug users take it for the same reasons, as it relieves pain and puts the recipient into a blissful state, but of course it has side effects for an addict.

During this fortnight, I would see Robert do things that I could never have imagined him doing, saying things that were definitely not him, and I would have to be reassured by the nurses that the effects were normal and that Robert would get through this.

One of the side effects would be uncontrollable scratching. Scratching his lips and skin until they bled. He would think there were mosquitos in the room that were biting him and he had to scratch them. He would be full of scabs like a drug addict and at first I would be constantly asking him to stop scratching but the nurses told me that it wouldn't work, to bear with it and that he wasn't hurting himself.

He would also think he was Spiderman, that he could spray webs from his wrists to climb the walls. Thankfully, he did not climb the walls, and there were many conversations, even selfies he would take whilst in this state. He basically did not sleep for the two weeks, only nap for 5 to 10 minutes at a time every hour.

Watching my husband go through this was scary. He was not the man that I married and it killed me some days to watch him act out like he was a drug addict. My therapy to get through was to ring a friend as I left the hospital and tell them what I saw and heard. I would be crying on the phone or cry myself to sleep most nights, just wishing this time would end soon. The nurses and ward doctor would tell me every day that they weren't worried about Robert's reactions, but what I saw was very distressing and because we did not want any other visitors there, only I would have the memory of that time.

After two weeks on the painkillers, Robert's immune system started to kick in, his mouth started to improve, and he was able to come off the drugs. But this wasn't the end of Robert's side effects.

On the 23rd of December, two days before Christmas, I noticed that Robert started to have shortness of breath, he asked for oxygen and within an hour his heart rate was increasing quickly whilst his blood pressure was dropping.

The doctors rushed in and started to check everything out and, within 30 minutes, a team of two doctors and four nurses were by his side and had made the decision to remove his internal line that had been inserted into his chest. The doctors told me that Robert must have an infection in his blood that has come from his line and they must pull it out immediately. While I am standing by the door, I heard the doctors counting down, "Three, two, one, Robert, take a big breath in". Within a few seconds the line was pulled out of Robert's chest and a doctor quickly applied pressure on the area for 30 minutes to stem the blood flow.

Once they had stitched up the hole, they took an x-ray of Robert's chest and found his lungs were clouded over to the point that you could not see his ribs. Robert's lungs were now starting to fail and urgent medication was to be given. The team of doctors and nurses that were looking over him had increased and they were distributing medication every hour. It was scary to watch my husband sitting there with oxygen flowing in to help him breath and I could see the fear in his eyes during every breathe.

Within an hour the doctors sedated Robert and was now being monitored every five minutes. At 7 p.m. the doctor told me that there was nothing more I could do and that I should go home, get some rest. It was going to be a long night for Robert and they told me that if he made it past midnight, he would most likely live and if things did not pick up, they would call me. Going home, sitting with mum and dad, waiting for the clock to tick around to midnight was horrible. The unknown of what was happening was intense and when I went to bed at 1am I was exhausted but a little relieved. I had not received a phone call so I was hoping that when the morning came Robert would be alive to fight another day.

I phoned the hospital at 6 a.m. and was told that Robert had gotten through the night and the signs were good. He was slowly improving and they said I would see a remarkable difference when I came in to see him. I raced into the hospital immediately and I could not believe what I saw when I came to Robert's room. Robert was sitting up in bed and as we embraced happy tears flowed down both of our cheeks. He was going to be ok and I never wanted to live through another night like that again. Christmas Eve was going to be a happy one and when the carols singers came through the ward, I sang the carols with them.

Christmas Day 2014 was a happy day in some ways. Robert was on the road to recovery, he was starting to eat more, drink more, the fluid that he was holding in his body was decreasing and he was able to walk between his bed and bathroom. Something he hadn't been able to do in weeks.

But for Robert, being in hospital was depressing, sad and not part of his plan. Seeing my husband lying in a bed that he did not want to be in was so sad and it was the hardest Christmas we had ever had together. No Christmas cheer, only tears and a desperation to get out of that environment. Nothing could change his demeanour, despite my best efforts.

It was heartbreaking, to the point that I remember going to the bathroom after unwrapping one of his presents for him and crying uncontrollably. His anger and sadness were getting to him and of course I had to bear the brunt of it. My parents came in to see Robert that day, only for a short time, but enough to lift some of the burden off me. I would sit with Robert for 10 hours that day, a day of sadness and we decided that we would not celebrate Christmas until Robert got home.

At home on Christmas night, we did not have a Christmas dinner, we did not open presents, we kept it all waiting for Robert to get home. Although the calendar said the 25th of December, we did not feel like celebrating. We did have a Christmas drink, more of a relaxant to end the day and hope that Robert's stay in hospital would come to an end soon. Robert had been in hospital since the 22nd of November, and for some traumas this is not long, but it was a long time for us!

The challenge had been set by the doctors that for Robert to be discharged he had to walk the ward by himself without oxygen and be able to eat three full meals a day. If he were able to achieve this in the next five days, his goal would be to go home from hospital on New Year's Day. What a wonderful start to the New Year!

The one thing I know about my husband is that when you set him a challenge, he will go after it. Robert was determined to start the new year at home, but to get there he not only had to build his strength but fight the demons in his head after being in hospital for five weeks.

To help him through this, my parents would go to the hospital in the morning, I would go in the afternoon and together we would get him through the next five days. As we took each slow step around the ward, me holding a 10-kilogram oxygen bottle, the nurses would ask if Robert was ok and then smile and say keep going, you will get there. Every day we walked further for longer and at home my parents were spring cleaning the house to ensure Robert would not be at risk of getting an infection.

On New Year's Eve, we got the clearance from the doctors that Robert had achieved the goals and he could go home tomorrow. After taking down the kids' drawings, collecting several gifts people had sent Robert, I went home a little earlier. I remember getting home having some dinner and having a champagne with mum and dad. As we clinked glasses and made a toast to Robert, we thought about the last six weeks that had tested all of us.

I also felt I was changing. I felt that my mental strength to be able to get through the dark hours had stepped up a level, but that night the tears flowed. Tears of happiness that Robert would be home again, tears of exhaustion that the relentless routine going to the hospital every day for six weeks was over and tears of joy that Robert was alive. Yes alive! He still had quite a difficult road in front of him, we can say that now, but, on New Year's Eve 2014, none of that mattered. My parents and I celebrated knowing that tomorrow was a new year, a new day, a new beginning for Robert.

Going to the hospital the next day, you could not wipe the smile off my face. I had a spring in my step and I was going to bring home the love of my life. Robert was sitting dressed ready to go. His happiness to be leaving was more "get me out of here", rather than joy. He was still very weak but was putting on a very brave face. He was very frail, only weighing 78 kilograms, 12 kilograms lighter than his prehospital weight. He had little hair and his face still bared the pain of the last six weeks. On the outside he was not the man that I had married but on the inside he certainly was. Pure grit and determination had got him to this day.

The coming days were mainly a lot of rest and minimal activity. For the first 100 days after a bone marrow transplant, even though the patient is allowed home, Robert had to visit the hospital three times a week, have blood tests, blood transfusions if needed and see the doctor at least once a week.

Robert's diet was extremely important for his recovery. He wasn't allowed to eat soft cheeses, deli meats, any processed foods and we were not allowed to have takeaways except for fish and chips or hamburgers. He was not allowed to go to the shops and the only trips we would have was a drive to a park and have some fish and chips for lunch making sure we stayed away from other people. Everything else was made from scratch with wholesome foods to prevent Robert from getting an infection or developing any stomach problems. I would clean the house constantly, wash towels every couple of days, ensure I did not touch Robert's toothbrush, anything that may spread infection.

Even though I was off work for another six weeks, the days just flew by. I was constantly keeping everything clean and driving Robert to appointments. I did not see this as a chore as I wanted my husband to live a long life without any further complications. He had been through so much and I did not want him to suffer anymore. So, the tasks were done in a loving way and it felt good being able to do them for him.

After Robert was home for about five days, his dad and brother came up to visit. It also saw the return home of my mum and dad. I had been so thankful for the time they had given up, the help and support they had given both of us but especially me. They had been my rock through this and I would not have gotten through it without them. It was sad to see them go but I just couldn't manage having too many people in the house at one time.

When Robert's dad and brother came through the door and first saw him it was confronting. Imagine seeing your son/brother bright and active, running around with your grandkids three months ago and the next visit only having the strength to walk 20 steps. There were lots of tears shed and sadness in that first day and I really felt for Robert's dad and how he was feeling. To allow them their privacy I sat outside until Robert needed me. I didn't want to intrude on their time together and ensure they shared the love they had for Robert.

As I watched the three Gomes men interact that week, it felt like a time that no one can take away. They have never spent this much time together as father and sons since they were kids and it was amazing to witness that. I have a photo of the three them when we went out for fish and chips. It is a photo I will cherish forever as I know Robert held this moment close to his heart.

After his father and brother returned to Melbourne, Robert and I had four weeks to ourselves. Robert continued to gain strength and our routines to the hospital saw us meeting several people who had just gone through the transplant too. Robert would have the same appointment time with a few people, one of them being his hospital neighbour Rob, and this allowed him to talk about his journey in hospital with people of like experiences. I was so grateful sitting by his side hearing him talk as it became a counselling session for him and his new friends. It was also nice for me to meet several wives that had also been by their husbands' sides through the transplant. Knowing you were talking the same language as someone else, makes communicating and comparing so much easier.

On the flip side, we would also see people disappear. You would say goodbye one day and then possibly never see them again. We did not have to ask most times where they had gone, they usually had passed over, unfortunately not being able to win the battle. I remember someone telling me that only 45 per cent of people survive a bone marrow transplant. A number would not return home, a number wouldn't make the 100-day milestone and a number wouldn't make it through the first year. It was part of the process, and I had to rationalise the statistics and would say to myself that Robert would not be one of those numbers.

During this time, I would also think of work. I had put my career on hold to care for my husband and if that put my role or future career at risk, then I was ok with that. Robert was my everything and although many people from work would contact me through this period, I did not want to talk about work as it was not part of my priorities right now. My only wish was that if I could play a role in Robert's life that gets him through this than nothing else in the world mattered.

Through this process we did meet two incredibly special couples. As I mentioned previously, Rob, who was Robert's next-door room buddy and had his transplant eight days before Robert. Rob and his wife Claire had been in the leukaemia system for five years, and after relapse needed a transplant. They lived in Brisbane and had two teenage sons.

Another buddy was Richard and his wife Heinke. We met Richard in the waiting room during the 100 days post-transplant. Richard had had his transplant 12 days after Robert and he and Heinke were such a vibrant couple. They lived in the Mary Valley two hours north of Brisbane on acreage and through Richards treatment had needed to live at one of the Leukaemia Foundation Villages in Brisbane. He wasn't allowed home for nearly 12 months. Richard also had the same doctor as Robert so the guys appointments would be one after the other.

The thing that we had in common with both couples was our ability to laugh. To always find something to chat about that bought happiness during uncertain times. Sometimes other people would frown at us and thought the laughter was a sign of disrespect. But some days laughter was the only way you got through those hours. The hours of sitting with people that you did not know, and unfortunately knew that possibly them or their loved ones were not going to survive.

During this time off work, two dear friends, Di and Tina, took me out to lunch. It was the first time I had been out for a meal without Robert for a few months. For me to go out for a meal I needed to have someone sit with Robert, which was our friend, John, Di's husband.

Most of the conversation was not about Robert which I was happy about, I wanted this to be a normal happy lunch. But what I did realise is that I had become so isolated from the rest of the world that I felt that I couldn't contribute to the conversation because I didn't know what they were talking about. My whole world had become Robert.

Hospitals, and bone marrow transplants that I did not know what to contribute. But I drifted back into the conversation and it was a great couple of hours away from my current life. I was incredibly lucky to have some beautiful girlfriends that cared and supported me through this time.

During the first 100 days after the transplant I do not remember Robert being frustrated. He seemed to cope well and he motivated himself by going for short walks and was building back his pre-transplant strength. We had several friends dropping in to say hello. They were always wanting to come and see Robert, making sure he was ok and lend a helping hand if we needed it. It was a time where I started to think about the friendships that I valued, the people that would care and love us unconditionally.

Chapter 5

The Power of Social Media

At the start of Robert's illness, a friend set up a private Facebook page to enable his close friends to send him messages of support, love, and hope. We had so many friends that wanted to know how Robert was going and I couldn't ring or text 100 people every day, so the site was perfect for updating on Robert's progress.

I found that through the hard times the Facebook page gave me an outlet to post quotes of courage, resilience, strength, and friendship. I could post a quote of how I was actually feeling, or what I needed for Robert and I to get through.

Over the last week of Robert's life, it also became a source of memories. Our friends posted their favourite stories and pictures of Robert. I could read them to Robert when he was in palliative care so he knew that everyone was thinking of him and the happy memories they cherished.

When Robert died it was also the place, I would upload the news. I was able to communicate a message to a large group quickly. These 30 or so close friends had been on this rollercoaster with us, and many, due to distance, had watched and heard through the words that I uploaded on Facebook.

At times the site would also make me angry. On a few occasions I would over obsess on who was commenting, who was liking and start to think that maybe some of the people we loved, that had been asked to be on this site, were not really interested or cared about us. I would ask myself questions on why they couldn't take five minutes out of their busy lives to acknowledge our battle.

Now, whether this was a fair assumption or not, during some periods when you are just getting through every day, just being the robot, just following the routine, just making sure you do not lose your shit, it did matter.

Social media outside of Robert's site was even harder. There were days that I didn't look at it, and days where I would over obsess in it. I sometimes wanted to live vicariously through someone else's life, other times I was hating everything they put up.

I would be happy for them when achievements and accomplishments were happening in their lives, and I would hate them for it at the same time. In my mind, I could not understand how they could be so happy when we were fighting for Robert's life. How dare they want to share their happiness and throw it in my face when I am just getting by.

What really started to annoy me were the hate comments, the "why me" comments. The complaining "oh, the traffic was so bad" or "the train was cancelled", or the sarcastic "what a great start to my day" comments. All I would be thinking was that they should try waking up for six weeks with no husband in your bed because he is in hospital fighting for his life and today I am going to sit there next to him, when he is doped out on meds. All the time I smile through it, saying tomorrow will be better. Where was my post saying "what a shit start to my day".

I know carers or people dealing with trauma will agree with how I was feeling. Social media can make it easier for you to communicate but can make you angry when your world is falling apart.

When other people's happiness is being shared for all to see, what do you do? do you ignore it, do you embrace it? There were days where I didn't comment or like their posts. But the thought that continually went through my head was, "When will it be our time to be happy again". When will Robert and I enjoy our lives free of treatment and start to post our beautiful photos of holidays and days out again?

Social media had its positives and negatives. I did not expect the emotional response I felt during the challenging days. I am grateful that it made life easier for me, and I have had to learn to put the device down when it gets to me. I am grateful that we live in an age where access to information and your loved ones is only a click away. It relieved the burden of having to make continuous phone calls every day when what I really needed was to recoup my energy.

Chapter 6

Life after Transplant

When it was time for me to return to work, Robert had not reached his 100 days post-transplant. This meant he still needed to have a carer 24/7 and had to visit the hospital three times a week. I had had three months off work caring for Robert and he had encouraged me to go back and resume my working life.

Robert's parents came up to stay with us for five weeks. I had never spent this much time with them before, and for me it was a time where I would get to know them more and would be grateful for them coming to care for their son.

Robert's mum was great. She cooked all the meals, and having an Anglo-Indian mother-in-law meant we were well cared for with delicious food. Sweet, aromatic spices wafted through our home daily, and Robert's mum showed me how to cook several different meals. I would go off to work every day and having them there meant I could have time to get back into my running, which was important for me to clear my head either before or after work and not have to worry about Robert. Robert's dad has a great sense of humour, so there was always lots of comedy happening in the kitchen.

Robert's parents would go to the hospital and sit with him. When Robert had to have his bone marrow aspiration, a procedure that nearly made Robert's dad passed out, they were there to help Robert through it but also understand what Robert had been through over the last 18 months.

The most special day we spent together was Robert's 43rd birthday. It was lovely to see his parents spoiling him, making his favourite meal, watch him cut his cake and just be there to celebrate a birthday again. I did not know whether Robert was going to have another birthday and having him share it with three of the people he loved the most melted my heart. Good things can come out of challenging events and the bond the four of us made over those five weeks would strengthen our relationship through the more challenging times.

I had been a little anxious going back to work. One, because I was leaving Robert at home and two, I had not worked for three months and would be returning to a project, not my nominal role. Day one back at work was exciting. Most of it was updating everyone on Robert's progress, them welcoming me back and saying how much they missed me. It was a good feeling which unfortunately did not last long.

The pressure of work and balancing Robert's routine was hard. I did not really like what I was doing at work and my colleagues, mostly men, did not really have the emotional IQ to ask how I was. So, most of the time I felt isolated and stayed quiet. Many of the conversations we had during meetings felt intolerable. I could not believe that people were getting worked up about stupid things that in my mind did not matter. I also could not believe how many people could not make a decision quickly and seeing that what we did wasn't life and death most days it just frustrated me to no end.

Through the last 18 months I had become particularly good at multi-tasking. At balancing everything in our lives. Now I was sitting in long winded meetings, talking about topics that could have been resolved on email and listening to people that just loved to hear their own voices. It was a real challenge for me and some days I would come home crying, wanting to resign and do something meaningful.

But I was not a quitter and although I spoke to my manager a lot about leaving, three months after returning he put me on a well-meaning project, something I could own and if I delivered would be great for the organisation. I started to work with a great team, some of them chosen by me and work started to become a place that I loved again. It made it a lot easier on Robert to see me coming home from work happy and reduced the strain in the house and on our marriage.

The next few weeks, which turned into months, were a basic routine. I would visit the hospital with Robert a couple of times a week. He had blood tests and treatments to ensure his numbers were tracking in the right direction. Most of the time all signs were good, the doctor would then reduce the medications which pleased Robert immensely, especially seeing that he left the hospital taking 35 tablets a day. It also pleased me as it meant I did not have to organise medication to that volume every day as well.

Robert took six months off work and as it came closer to for him to return, he was getting excited. Excited to enter the world again, to be able to return to a normal life that reflected the past and gave him a future. A future that was far away from leukaemia, far away from bone marrow transplants and into a world of hope and opportunity. I was a little anxious about Robert's return as he had not really understood the energy it would take. But I could not ask him to stay home any longer, he was going stir crazy and that had an impact on me too. So, the best thing for him was to ease back into work part time and build his hours over the next two months.

Our first holiday after Robert's bone marrow transplant was a road trip to Port Douglas. We took the trip with our friends John and Di. We stayed up in Port Douglas where we wined and dined. We also stayed in Mission Beach in an amazing beach front house where we relaxed, Robert fished, played cards and beach cricket, and went on walks.

But our trips had changed. Robert was now on a different mix of medications, ones that would cause him to suffer with water retention in his body and numbness in his feet. He would be fine in the mornings, walking and enjoying the sites but by the afternoon his feet were so blown up and sore that he would have to put his feet up and rest to enable him to go out to dinner that night. Now most people would love to have to go back to their hotel, literally put their feet up and watch the world go by. But when you have to do it every day to be able to make it out to dinner that night, it becomes quite frustrating, which it did for Robert.

We also had to be mindful that he could not be around people with colds or infections. We had to make sure we always ate good food and in the first 12 months he would be incredibly careful with the amount of alcohol he consumed. He slept a lot longer and he went through periods where he would just sit and take in the views and watch the world go by.

Before we went on this trip, we talked about what activities Robert wanted to do while we were away. One of these was to go fishing. Fishing in the sea. Fishing in the sea where crocodiles would sometimes be seen. So, while we were at Mission Beach, he took the opportunity to go surf fishing, to go out into the ocean to waist deep and try and bring in the one that did not get away.

While Robert was fishing, I sat in an armchair watching out for crocs and ensuring Robert didn't lose his footing and go under. That day was never about catching that huge fish, it was about seeing a man achieving his dreams and doing the things that he loved. Being able to witness this brought tears to my eyes, just watching him without fear in the ocean, having fun would not have been possible if he had not had the transplant.

Through the tears and the smile, I reminded myself how lucky I was to have married a man that had such strength and courage. Watching Robert doing one of the things he loved made me so proud and to think that 11 months ago he was in hospital having a bone marrow transplant and today he was fishing in the ocean.

Robert and I had been to many amazing countries in the world. We had seen many places that most of our family and friends will never see. But this road trip was one of the best holidays I had ever had. It was well-earned for both of us and to share it with our beautiful friends John and Di was so memorable for them to. It had been a rollercoaster ride over the last 12 months and to be able to live some sort of normality with my husband and best mates made me so happy and proud.

When you have a bone marrow transplant, it is like being re-born. The day you have your transplant, it will forever be remembered as your "second birthday". For Robert, his was the 28th of November. To celebrate his first rebirthday, we spent the weekend in Noosa. It was such a beautiful location, and by this time Robert had regained a lot of his strength and we were able to enjoy short walks on the beach, full range of foods and have a few drinks together. His feet would still swell with the medication but the routine of feet up in the afternoon was just part of his and our normal day. Taking this trip and celebrating this milestone was important.

2017 was a big year for us, too. It was the first year since Robert's treatment that we decided to start living our life via adventures. We visited our family and friends in Melbourne quite often and I had started to go on girls weekends and we decided to take a few trips with friends.

The biggest achievement was hiking 75 kilometres on the Overland Track at Cradle Mountain Tasmania. Over the last year our friends Heinke, Richard and Robert and I had started a group called Unplugged – Hike for Life. We gathered another five bone marrow stem cell survivors and a camera man to hike the track and bring hope for current and future patients that there is life after blood cancer. The camera man would film the six-day trek, create a documentary which could be viewed by patients, carers and family members.

Leading up to the event I was hiking up to 30 kilometres a week. Unfortunately, Robert's feet were still sore and aching so his preparation, you would say, was not ideal. But as you have heard Robert is a fighter, he would never let the team down and was determined to be a role model for future recipients.

In April 2017, we set off to Launceston and started the six-day trek. Within the first hour Robert was feeling the enormity of the hike. If you do not know about the hike, take a look. It is not for the faint hearted, most of our friends will never attempt it, yet here was this man proving a point to himself and others that he could finish it.

On day four, Robert injured himself and he was already struggling just to make it to the hut each night through his pain. After he injured himself, day five and six were a struggle for the both of us. I ended up taking Robert's pack and spent the rest of the walk crying several paces behind him, cursing him inside, asking myself why he was putting himself through this pain and suffering. But this man was not called Superman in awe by his nieces, nephews and godchildren for nothing. He proved that he really did have Superman powers, and on the last day of the hike, surrounded by his new friends, he led the team across the line.

If he could fall up the steps to the last hut, I know he would have. The exhaustion on our faces, the emotion of finishing such a tremendous feat was enormous. I was relieved that we had made it, but emotionally exhausted from the strength, resilience, and courage that I had had to bring to this hike to get us both through it.

As we sat at dinner that night, Robert struggling to walk to the restaurant, the happiness and elation began to kick in. We had conquered an adventure that I never thought Robert would ever be able to attempt much less complete. For the first time that day it all made sense as to why Robert wanted to achieve it. His pride, his passion, and his need to help others was why he pushed himself to do it. Plus, he wanted to achieve something that to him, felt like being normal again.

Pre and post that hike the group also had a goal of raising money for the Leukaemia Foundation. In November 2017, we were able to present a cheque to the foundation for $28,990. Our goal had been met for that event, which enabled us to gain the confidence and determination to raise more money for them over the next four years.

Over the three years since Robert had been diagnosed, we realised there was so much to be thankful for. There would be so many times when I would reflect on that period and I would think about how different life was before leukaemia. We were still enjoying life, but what we wanted to do had changed. Our ability to deal with these changes made us stronger as a couple. We were thankful for each other's love and never took for granted the life we had together.

Chapter 7

Confronting Anxiety

Before I experienced anxiety, I never knew what it was or how it would feel. I had heard people at work talk about anxiety attacks, but I didn't understand what they were. I am sure many people have anxious feelings; we may even refer to it as nervousness sometimes. Anxiety is different. Anxiety is when these anxious feelings don't go away. They are ongoing and happen without any reason or cause and it scares you because you don't know it is anxiety rather you may think you are about to die.

For me I started to experience anxiety after Robert had finished his treatment in February 2014. I was at work around 5 p.m. and I didn't have what I would call a stressful day. I was doing my email when I started to experience pins and needles in my left hand and my vision started to become blurry. But within minutes I started to panic. My breathing started to become shallow and my heart was racing. I had never experienced anything like this before and I didn't know what to do.

I called a colleague who was still at their desk and asked them to come into my office and talk to me. I knew I had to calm myself down, to try and regulate my heartbeat, and so I laid down on the floor and another colleague called an ambulance.

The symptoms I felt made me think I was having a heart attack. Not that I knew what a heart attack felt like. I had never had a heart attack before or hadn't experienced anyone having a heart attack. But a racing heart, pins and needles in the left arm and shallow breathing were symptoms of a heart attack so I assumed that was what was going on.

The paramedics checked my blood pressure, tested my sugar levels and diagnosed it as dehydration. I was not drinking enough water during the day and I was able to go home post drinking a litre of fluid. I really had to start looking after myself. I could not afford to have these sorts of episodes at work or around Robert. I did not need Robert to panic and then start worrying about me. He had been through enough. After this first episode, I did not realise that this was anxiety.

Within 12 months, the episodes started to become more regular. I had one when Robert was having his transplant, quite a few post Robert's transplants with most of them occurring at home during the night.

The anxiety attacks that consumed me at night were the worst. I would wake up sweating, heart racing. As I bolted upright in bed and placed my head between my legs, breathing deeply, trying to make it pass, I would be scared. Sometimes, I would have to wake up Robert and he would talk me through the episode until I would lay back sitting up and I would finally fall asleep. The night-time episodes would then make me lethargic and it would take a few days until I was feeling myself again.

I then had a serious episode at work. I was in a video conference and started to feel nauseas. I started eating my lunch but could feel my heart rate increasing. I refilled my water bottle thinking I needed more fluids and this would help,but it didn't and before I knew it, I could see my heart beating out of my chest. I told my colleagues in the room that something was wrong. I was clammy, feeling hot, had the shakes, my heart was out of control and I felt sick. My colleagues immediately disconnected the call, rang the ambulance, kept talking to me until the paramedics arrived and they took me to hospital. It was this episode, where I had ended up in the emergency room for the fourth time that the doctor said, there is nothing wrong with your heart. We would like you to read some information about anxiety and depression. Wow, anxiety.

I took their advice, saw my doctor, went on a low dose anti-depressant medication, and started to see a psychologist.

It was the assistance of the psychologist that really helped. She talked me through how to deal with the voices in my head that triggered the physical symptoms. We talked about my fears. My biggest one was what would happen to Robert if I died. Who would look after him if the leukaemia came back? How would he cope when we did not have kids to look after him? That we lived in Brisbane away from our family and friends and how would he cope with life in general without me. I also realised that the trauma, what I had seen and dealt with had affected me too and I had not recognised that.

My psychologist told me not to ignore the thoughts and feelings, as they were real, they were happening, but to rather address them and allow myself to move past them. I could do that without anyone knowing about it. My practice began with, "This is just a thought so acknowledge it, it is unnecessary and unhelpful, it is either negative, positive or neutral and nothing has happened previously".

Sometimes I would have to be persistent and say it multiple times to allow the thoughts to pass and overtime it would take less time to move the negative thoughts on. It took me over a year before the practice of addressing the thoughts and feelings became second nature.

Now this practice, plus a number of sessions working through the moments with my psychologist when I felt anxious, talking through the thoughts I was having that created the anxiety and doing a number of other practices started to have a positive effect on my life.

This enabled me to address the uncertainties in my life, which were only thoughts. Work through my husband's illness and the changes I had seen in him and help me to facilitate the conversations with my husband that were not being resolved. It enabled me to remove some of the general pressures in life and I had a period without anxiety attacks.

Another helpful practice that I also use is guided meditation. I have used different apps in the past four years that have different guided meditation sessions that are related to stress, managing anxiety, sleep, coping with cancer, sadness, grief, and the list goes on. I found that if I did them daily it would enable me to start to focus on the present moment and help to confront distraction from the devil voices in my head.

Even today I have not perfected guided meditation. Sometimes I do get distracted, sometimes I even fall asleep during it, but practicing these techniques allows me to create a peaceful mind and cope with the current challenges in life.

The one thing the medical staff taught me is that anxiety does not magically go away and that there will be further challenging times ahead. If I wanted to live a healthy mindful life, then I had to work out how I was going to do this, and dedicate time proactively to engage with mindful activity.

I learnt after Robert died that I had to look after myself even more than ever, especially now that I live by myself. There have been so many challenging days after he died, but I am thankful that engaging the psychologist during Robert's treatment has helped me to resolve any anxiety before it now becomes an episode.

Today, I am still on the anti-depressants and I have engaged a psychologist on and off. I am not scared to tell anyone that I needed help to calm the voices, to talk about my anxiety and call out for help when I need it.

This picture was taken on our trek in Tasmania, at a time when my anxiety was at its worst.

Chapter 8

The Reality of Relapse

One of the fears that every blood cancer or any kind of cancer patient has is the possibility of relapse and you think about it a lot. Robert's mate Rob, his neighbour during the transplant relapsed after his transplant. He went for a normal appointment and was told the blast cells (leukaemia cells) were back. He was rushed to hospital that day and we visited Rob and supported him, hoping to give him an extra level of strength to fight again which he did.

In August 2017, after the hike and a couple of holidays, Robert was in a good place. He was now only visiting his doctor every two months and on minimal medications. I remember the day so vividly when Robert was told he had relapsed.

I met Robert at the clinic and found him in the bone marrow biopsy room. He was sitting there waiting for the doctor and I said to him,

"To what do we owe the pleasure of being in this room today?" The nurses joked around saying comments like "only the best for Robert". But when the doctor arrived and closed the door, we knew something was up. Robert had had his blood tests the day before and in the results the blast cells had reappeared. All we heard from the doctor was that the leukaemia was back!

Both Robert and I broke down. It was nearly three years since Robert had had the transplant. The doctor then proceeded immediately to complete a bone marrow biopsy to confirm the results. Because Robert had a great rapport with the nurses at the clinic, so many dropped by the room in shock and could not believe it. Not Robert. Why was this happening? Robert did not deserve this.

It then came time for me to start making those dreaded calls again. First my parents, who were in Brisbane visiting, then Robert's parents, my brother, and my boss. Everyone that we spoke to or heard the news were devastated. I thought, this cannot be happening. But it was, and again our lives would be turned upside down.

After the appointment we went back home and my parents were there. They were in shock, did not know what to say. They were asking us what was next and at that point we did not know. It would take another week for the full report to come back, to understand how bad the relapse was and what treatment would be recommended. We all sat in the lounge room that afternoon not saying much but I knew our brains were all racing wanting to understand why. Why Robert?

The following week the results came back and confirmed the Acute Myeloid Leukaemia (AML) was back. Six per cent of Robert's cells were blast cells, leukaemia cells, and the next round of treatment would be to get him back into remission and then have further treatment to cure him. Robert's doctor told us that there were a few options to take and that a low strength dose of chemotherapy would be the first step.

Now it was back to multiple visits per week at the cancer clinic. The medical staff there were amazing and most of the visits were happy ones. We mostly saw the same people and would chat to them like they were our best friends. I have seen several people looking solemn which is understandable, their loved ones complaining about the time it took for treatment or how the doctor was running so late. But Robert and I are the type people that just took it in our stride and make the best of a bad situation.

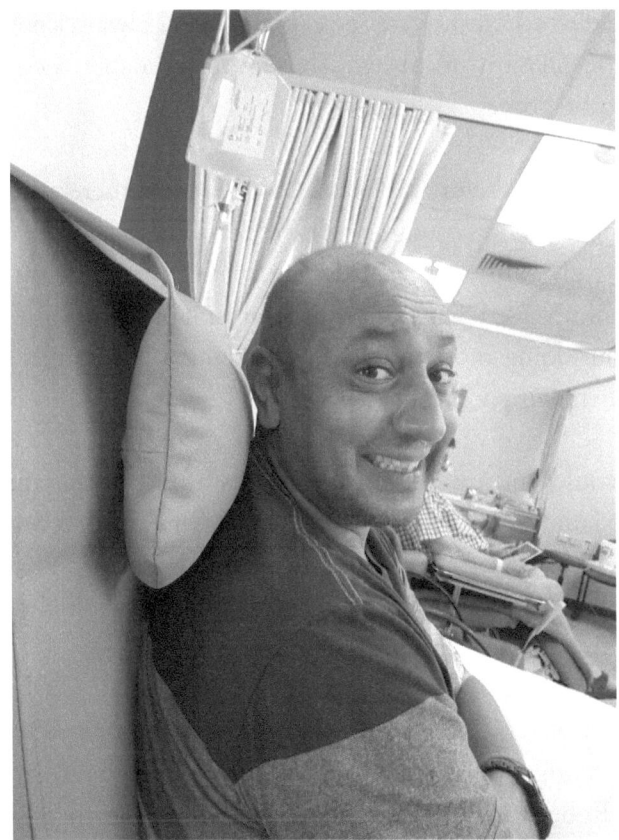

During the first round of chemotherapy Robert was admitted back to hospital for four days due to ongoing fevers. Whenever Robert was in hospital, he hated it. He was always looking for a way to be discharged, sometimes even trying to negotiate with the doctor and nurses. Everyone around him knew he hated it and he typically got discharged early, or earlier than other patients as his doctor always knew Robert recovered best at home.

Having Robert back in hospital was always a trying time for me. What Robert did not understand was that when he was released early than what I would have liked, it always increased my stress levels. I would have to rebalance my work, the house, whatever else was needed to accommodate the early release. I always knew Robert did not consider any of this, which is understandable, seeing he just wanted to be home.

In December, just before Christmas, we were told there were no blast cells in Robert's blood counts. It was the best Christmas present anyone could have given us. Robert had been coping with the dosages well, he had had no side effects since his stint in hospital and he was able to go about doing most things. Even having a few drinks here and there and enjoying Christmas Day.

Robert would end up having six rounds of chemotherapy during this period and in January we were told Robert was in remission. To hear those words was like being proposed to or saying "I do" on our wedding day. It always overwhelmed us and tears rolled down our faces. Again, another day of celebration.

In March 2018, with Robert in remission, we decided to go Melbourne to see our family and friends and for our god daughter's eighteenth birthday. Robert's birthday was also in March, so I arranged a surprise party for him. He was turning 46 which is not a milestone birthday, but when you are undertaking chemotherapy which restricts your ability to do a lot of things, a celebration with Robert's nearest and dearest was the perfect thing for us.

The party was on the last night we were in Melbourne and our family and friends kept it a surprise. Robert was so overwhelmed when he stepped through the doors and waiting for him to appear were around 60 people. Our parents, siblings, nieces, nephews, god children, friends and their children were all here to celebrate Robert's birthday.

The night was a big success filled with laughter, dancing and lots of reminiscing. Being around our family and friends, was not just therapy for Robert but also for me. My best friends were there, hugging me, loving me. I could not ask for a better group of friends that always made themselves available for us. Robert loved it and I am so happy that I had organised that night, as although I didn't know it at the time, it was the last birthday Robert would celebrate with his family and friends.

After we returned to Brisbane, Robert still off work on sick leave, we decided it was time to start searching for a new house. We had been in Brisbane for nine years and our house was great, in a wonderful suburb, but our dream had always been to have a property with land to build an accommodation business on. Something that would allow us to escape the hustle and bustle of suburbia and corporate life.

Since Robert's transplant, we had started to visit Richard and Heinke's property which was situated in the Mary Valley, two and half hours north of Brisbane. Those weekends were so relaxing and we started to want to spend more time up there.

After many weeks of looking online and Robert visiting several properties, we came across 35 acres with an existing house, sheds and the most incredible views. I was overwhelmed with the size of the house and the potential accommodation business. But seeing Robert's face light up and start talking about the things that he wanted to do to the property, the only thing we could do was buy it.

It seemed so surreal. Here we were living in suburbia, incredibly happy, and now sometime in the next nine months we would be moving to the country where I could finally start to see our next chapter of our life playing out. Robert was in remission, doing well, we were going to build our dream business and live happily ever after.

Just before we settled on the house, Robert started to feel fatigued again. He had not had any chemotherapy since March and we put it down to the latest trip to Melbourne and Robert was keeping busy undertaking a horticulture course. The blood tests in late June gave us the reason why - the blast cells were back again. He had leukaemia for the third time, second relapse. How much did we have to take, how many lessons still needed to be learnt and again, Why Robert?

This time Robert and his doctor decided to take a more evasive chemotherapy treatment where he was admitted to hospital and would be there for four weeks. The first week in hospital went well. He had minimal side effects, so Robert's doctor allowed him to go home after the last dose of chemotherapy. I was not terribly happy with this decision, but Robert was so damn stubborn. This was the trait I loved in him for fighting this dreaded disease but was also the trait that could frustrate me so much as it meant playing Russian roulette with this disease.

I was still working during this time as we had been through this before and although we had to go back to the clinic three times in that next week, I could still balance Robert and work from home. I would take my laptop into the clinic, put my earphones in, and undertake meetings, emails and phone calls whilst there.

Eight days out of hospital Robert started to get some significant side effects. He wasn't eating much; I was forcing down liquids and he was sleeping a lot. I was monitoring his temps and although they weren't high, I was getting quite worried.

In the early hours of the second week post-chemotherapy, Robert got up to go to the bathroom and crashed into the wall. I woke up suddenly and asked if he was ok. He told me that it was too dark in the room and he could not see the wall. But I could see the walls so I quickly jumped out of bed as Robert opened the door to the ensuite and within the next second he grabbed the glass shower, lost his balance, and fell to the floor. As I got into the ensuite I quickly grabbed his head as he went down which prevented him from knocking himself out. Even though he was conscious, he was in a bad way and it was awful to see him in such a state. A grown man with the stubbornness of a bull was now lying helplessly in a small ensuite.

The thought of that morning brings tears to my eyes today. For many days, I wished Robert had not hid his true symptoms and stopped being the fighter that everyone loved. His courage would at times cause significant pain on him and me and now I had to look down at my husband on the tiles, not able to move and apologising for what had happened.

The only thing I knew what to do in these situations was to take a deep breath and help him out. Robert was around 75 kilograms at this time, so moving him when he was a dead weight and cannot move himself was quite a feat. After moving him back to sit back on the toilet, I rang the ambulance. The ambulance took him back to the hospital where he went into emergency. When I arrived, his doctor came in and told me Robert was severely dehydrated and after taking a number of tests was transferred back to the ward.

Robert was in a bad way and I wasn't going to be able to balance work and Robert. I needed to be 100 per cent with my husband, everything in my world would have to be put on hold. So I made the decision to take time off work and support Robert through this next challenge. Thankfully, my manager supported me again by putting someone into my role, someone that I trusted and the only thing that mattered and took up my time was Robert.

Through several tests, the doctors told us that Robert had a liver infection. His kidneys were not functioning as well as they should and the infections were having a negative impact on his heart. This instigated the highest antibiotic regime that can be administered and increasing Robert's fluid intake to push the infections through. After a few days, Robert's heart and kidneys started to go back to normal, but the doctors were still concerned about his liver.

But 29 days after the initial chemotherapy Robert's liver results were going in the wrong direction. His doctor ordered a liver biopsy and by this time Robert was having fevers (temps over 38 degrees) every six hours. He was not sleeping and the fluid in his legs was giving him tremendous pain. The doctors administered more drugs for the liver which meant Robert would be in hospital for another three weeks. He was not happy but it was either three weeks there or his liver could fail and he could die.

This was now the third time I had been told that things were touch-and-go. While I was trying to be brave for my husband and not show how worried I was, Robert was extremely upset. He did not have the strength to get out of bed, but he had the strength to tell me that he wasn't giving up. He would continue to fight and I promised I would be by his side every day until he was well enough to go home. These were highly stressful times. Battling this disease was one thing, but having to ask your loved one if he can keep doing this, does he still want to live and then promising that I would do anything for him to ease his pain was extremely hard to watch.

As the days went by over the next three weeks, I completed the same daily routine. Get up, have breakfast, play with the dog, either do errands, clean up the house or cook my dinner for the next few nights. I had a stringent routine and knew it was important to eat right, sleep enough and do some exercise. I would then go into the hospital around midday. I always wanted to be there for lunch and stay until around 7:30 p.m. when Robert was tired. I sometimes stayed longer if things were not going good for him. I wanted to be by his side when he needed me.

This was also a time where I was not able to have my parents by my side. I would keep everyone updated daily either by text or phone. I also updated everyone on our private Facebook page. Again, this allowed me to provide updates without having to call everyone every couple of days. Repeating the same story can be extremely draining and I needed all my energy for what Robert and I were dealing with.

As Robert started to improve, his patience with being in hospital and being sick was wearing thin. The only person that would bear the brunt of that frustration was me. We had been waiting for Robert's immune system to kick in for over 30 days. Every time Robert had chemotherapy it seemed that his immune system was not reacting as quickly as previous times. So, every day for at least the last 20 days I had been saying, "Do not give up hopefully your immune system will come back tomorrow", and then I would repeat that the next day, and the next.

By around day 40, the tension between Robert and I got to boiling point. Robert and I rarely fought. We always seem to get through the hard times but this day was not one of them. I told Robert, "It's ok, your numbers will come back in the next few days", and then Robert just lost it. He told me he was sick and tired of hearing the same thing every day, that the numbers were not coming back. That I was annoying him with my stupid words of hope and positivity, that the situation was shit, he hated being here.

By this stage I had had enough of his attitude as well. I told him that I felt so sorry for him, that he was in this position, but why couldn't he understand that the doctors had told him that he wasn't getting out of hospital for at least another ten days and he had to put up with that because it was too dangerous for him to leave. Then he told me to go. That I was not helping him and he wanted me to leave. On hearing this, I slammed down my laptop on the bed and said, "Fine, I will." By now, I was crying and so upset at how he could be so rude to me. Why was he saying these things and why did he continually take it out on me?

So, with that, I picked up my bag and left. I did not know where I was going, all I knew is that Robert had to learn a lesson. I knew he was hurting so much, that he was so angry and frustrated but I was not going to be his punching bag today. I was hurting and was so frustrated, but we had to work through this together, not start attacking each other. For the next 30 minutes I went and got a coffee and sat in the waiting room.

While I was away, I received several calls from Robert, which I didn't answer. He had to understand that he had hurt me and I know I might have frustrated him but I was only trying to help him. Although Robert was asking me to come back to the room to talk, I ignored the messages and waited until I was calm enough to go back.

Once back in the room we embraced each other and we both started crying, Robert apologising for what he had said to me, and me for not thinking about what my words were doing to him. Together we agreed that this positive attitude approach was not working. It was not the reality, things were shit, this time in hospital had been shit and we were both having a really hard time.

We agreed that there were to be no more fake words. We would be honest with each other, honest about how we were feeling and over the next ten days our new approach worked. It allowed both us to just take each minute, moment, day with a sense of reality and eased the tension to basically zero between us. That is not to say it wasn't hard, it was extremely hard to continue to see Robert fighting, but the honesty and different mindset was sending him in the right direction.

After 54 days, Robert was released from hospital. What an amazing day. Robert, Jonty (our dog) and I were back together as a family again. All of Robert's numbers were back to normal and although his physical recovery would take quite a few more weeks, he was happy again and ready to take on the world.

Those eight weeks had given me a new perspective. I decided I was going to be more honest with my family and friends about Robert's situation. I was also going to be more honest about how I was feeling. How I was coping. I was going to ask for help. If my parents cannot come up then I need more from others. I always thought I could get through anything but these eight weeks taught me that I had to put some serious routines in place focusing on my mental health.

During Robert's time in hospital another major milestone had occurred in Robert's life. We both worked for the same corporate and Robert had now been off work for nearly 12 months whilst relapsing twice. The company had announced reductions and several redundancies would be available and Robert was offered one of them. Robert had had 28 years in this company, although over the last five years he had been at work for only three of those. You never want to leave a company, a job and people that you love working with. But it was time and it would make a difference when it came to Robert's outlook on life and what he was working towards.

For me, it was a huge relief. I did not have to worry about Robert thinking it would be possible for him to go back to work. Robert had been through so much and I saw the implications of that. Robert would not have been the same at work. He had to work so hard to remember things as the chemotherapy had affected his memory.

One thing I had to continually remember to do was allow Robert to achieve things in life that made him feel good. I had to let Robert do the things and allow him to turn it into an accomplishment. I had to learn not to criticise him if it was not done 100 per cent, or if he forgot to do them. The other thing that Robert and I had agreed was that I would not tell him if he repeated himself three times about the same thing. If he got to the fourth time, I would subtly say to him, thanks Robert I think you may have already told me that. Then he would know it was the fourth time. Most times it did not get to that, but again it meant that we just had to devise a way that Robert would not have to worry about it. It usually meant writing things in a diary which Robert would check every day so he knew what he needed to do.

Now we were in the second week of September, and in the next few weeks our god-daughter Caitlin would be coming up with her friend for her 16th birthday. We were taking her to Sea World to swim with the dolphins, Movie World and Australia Zoo. It was going to be another week of creating amazing memories for all of us and putting the last ten weeks behind us. Robert had regained some strength but not enough to do all the activities with us. But we had an awesome week, spoilt our god daughter who was so grateful for everything we did.

The Reality of Relapse

On the last day of them visiting us in Brisbane, we participated in Light the Night, a charity event run by the Leukaemia Foundation to raise vital funds for their organisation. It is a gathering of families, friends, people who have been affected by blood cancer and those who are still affected, or for those remembering loved ones that are now our angels.

Robert held a white lantern during the event. The white lantern recognises people living or have lived with blood cancer. Family and friends walk with blue lanterns and yellow lanterns are for family and friends that have lost a loved one. It starts off with a ceremony remembering all who have been affected. We heard from a couple of survivors and then we lit the lamps in order of yellow, white and blue and walked the 3 kilometres remembering Robert's journey.

We had several friends participate in 2018. I remember two beautiful moments on that night. One was when a stranger came up to Robert and said, "Good luck mate, hope you continue to live a wonderful life." The second was when we were walking. I was walking in front of Robert and I looked behind and saw Robert in the middle with his white lantern while our friends surrounded him with their blue ones. It was like we had created a protective barrier around him, a line of protection and love. My heart hurts when I remember that moment, but seeing Robert walking with his friends, smiling and having a great time was amazing. This was so typical of Robert. He would never give up when it came to supporting his mates. He was always doing things for others and doing it for the cause that he believed would save his life.

Life after the last ten days was starting to feel like it was going in the right direction. We were now undertaking twice weekly visits to the clinic, mostly to receive a bag of platelets and sometimes red blood cells. Robert's system had really taken a beating so it was going to take some time to produce his cells himself. Robert had undergone a bone marrow biopsy in September and the results had been positive and Robert was in remission.

Again, this was short lived as by the middle of October we were presented with a different set of results. The blasts were back for the fourth time. This was now looking like Robert had relapsed for the third time in 14 months. It was devastating to say the least.

Although Robert did not seem to react in the same way as me and was playing it down. He told people that the Doctor said there were blast cells present but there is nothing to worry about. He was interpreting the doctors message quite differently to me and I did not understand why. But when Robert had his next set of tests four weeks later it was confirmed that Robert had relapsed. So, the discussions then went to what was next and the good news was that Robert still had options. That there were still a few more procedures that could be undertaken before the river had dried up!

Over the coming weeks and as we approached Christmas, several doctors reviewed Robert's case and started to make recommendations on what procedure he could have. In the meantime, the blast cells had increased and the doctors needed to have them brought down before they could begin those options.

Although there were options the survival rates were not good. We were nearing the last resort action and it was very worrying for both of us. Up until this point Robert's haematologist never discussed the odds and we never wanted to know them either. Not knowing them allowed Robert to just focus on the here and now, and I did not worry about playing the numbers game. But now, it was time to be honest and know the challenge ahead.

Over the next four weeks as we headed towards Christmas 2018, we had my parents back up again and enjoyed a lot of happy times. Although we continued to have twice weekly appointments at the clinic and the numbers were rising a little, they were still in a place where chemotherapy did not have to be started.

We also moved into our new house a week before Christmas. Just before we moved Robert had started to lose feeling in his feet and pain in his knee. He had several tests and his doctor gave him strong pain medications to relieve the pain. Thankfully when we were packing up the house to move, we had our eldest god daughter Abby up to help. Her and I would pack the boxes at night, cart them up and down the stairs while Robert would sit on the lounge, resting his legs. He just was not able to go up and down those 25 stairs without extreme pain.

I was so thankful that Abby was with us during this time. She got me through some nights where I could have let loose at Robert. I would get so frustrated with him that he was not acknowledging his situation. That he was trying to do everything that a normal able human being would do, or maybe like any man would, but he could not! He was just making his situation worse. I would tell him to only do what he was capable of. But Robert thought he was invincible, that he could do anything, especially everything I could do, and I could see it just was not possible.

We moved into our house on the 18th of December 2018 and it was an amazing day. We cleaned up the old house ready for handover and started the next chapter of our life. Thankfully, because I had a national team, I was not constrained to working out of Brisbane and the company had several locations on the Sunshine Coast that I could work out of. It also allowed me to be close to Robert if he needed me and not tire me out from the long drives.

The Christmas period was a good time, enjoyed with friends, both old and new. John and Di came up for Christmas and with them we spent Boxing Day with Richard and Heinke. We had a couple of down days where Robert would be frustrated that he could not stay up as late with friends. He also hated having to rest when in the garden with me, but overall, we had a wonderful three weeks together enjoying the serenity of our new home, planning numerous projects and dreaming about the life we were going to build together.

**One of the last days we worked together on our property.
It was here that I learnt how to use a chainsaw.**

Chapter 9

Pressure and Pain

Over January, Robert's blast counts were still stable and we were waiting to hear from the doctors as to whether his original donor was able to donate her cells again and Robert would have them infused. By the third week in January we found out that Robert's donor was willing to donate her cells, but what I also started to find was that Robert just did not have the energy to do the things that he wanted to. He also was not keeping his fluid intake up enough to be able to cope with the Queensland heat.

We still did the trips into Brisbane for Robert's clinic appointments. The nurses made it a little easier by making times that meant we did not have to get up too early to get to the clinic. By this time Robert needed at least ten hours of sleep a night. So leaving home around 9 a.m. for a two-hour drive allowed Robert to be more on top of his day and allowed me to do some work before we left home.

In early February, Robert's blast cell count started to rise significantly and on the afternoon of the 13th of February we received the phone call from the doctor that because Robert's blast cells had increased, they could not do the donor infusion and that we will need to speak to Robert's haematologist about alternative chemotherapy.

Robert and I looked at each other in sheer disbelief, thinking what the hell? No, this cannot be happening. Robert's instant response was, "This is not right, we need to get on to my haematologist and find out what is going on." We were so disappointed. Robert said there must be a mistake, the results cannot have doubled in the last week. This isn't possible. My doctor will fix it. He always does!

Unfortunately, the results were right, Robert was now outside the boundaries of the donor infusion treatment. How many knock downs did Robert have to endure to get the right outcome? We were both so upset. It felt like the world was against us. I would ask out loud, what lesson do we have to learn, why us, why Robert. Every time we saw light at the end of the tunnel it was like it was teasing us. But we were not greedy people, all we wanted was happiness via a cure.

But as usual after the initial 24 hours of sadness, anger, and disbelief, we mounted that horse again and decided to fight. Well, Robert decided to fight another fight and I decided to stand by my man. Now we were entering the 15th round of chemotherapy. Yes, 14 rounds had been completed, probably amounting to approximately 120 doses of chemotherapy. It is quite extraordinary to think that Robert had had to endure that much poison and he was still willing to give it another go.

This time around, Robert would start off with the low dose chemotherapy and an oral chemotherapy drug. The only downer was that Robert would have to spend his birthday in hospital and I was going to be away for work. I had never been away for any of

Pressure and Pain

Robert's hospital stays, but Robert insisted that I take the trip that this procedure is straight forward, you're in Sydney and only an hour by plane if you need to get back. I also had my parents back up in Brisbane, so I felt a little better knowing that. I arranged for a few friends to visit to try and make his birthday a little bit special. But Robert did not care about that. He just wanted these five days to go as quickly as possible so he could get back to the farm and start the next phase of his treatment.

Robert's body accepted the new drugs without any initial side effects, but what we were starting to see was an escalation of the pain in his legs. It seemed that as the body became accustomed of this new poison that was killing the blast cells, his pain in his legs was escalating out of control. Robert's pain threshold is high, he rarely complained and always tried to bare the pain by taking minimal pain medications. It was his bravery and courage to fight through the worst pain that always got him through. But not this time.

One night in March 2019, I was sitting on the couch watching TV. Robert had gone to bed early when I started to hear a noise. At first, I thought it was the neighbours' cows mooing, so I put the tv on mute and I heard the groaning again. It took me a few seconds to realise it was Robert. I ran to the bedroom and I found Robert holding his knee just saying, "The pain, the pain, I cannot deal with this pain." I quickly got out the pain medication and gave him the maximum dose. Unfortunately, the medication took around 20 to 25 minutes to take effect, so for that time, Robert was in excruciating pain.

He was crying, and I was trying to hold it together whilst asking Robert to move into different positions to ease the pain but nothing was working. The pain on Robert's face was so hard to witness that we just had to work through this episode. I had never seen him like this, it was the worst pain I had ever seen him in.

What started to happen after this episode was that Robert would experience onsets of the same pain every two hours. It felt like we had just got to sleep before the episodes would start again. The worst episodes of this acute pain would strike at night. He was also having trouble walking due to the neuropathy in his feet and legs and he was now having to use a walking stick to keep his balance. He hated using the walking stick. He would tell me that he felt like an old man, but I didn't care what he looked like as it was for his own safety.

This time, it was really getting to me. I was trying to balance caring for Robert and working. Even though my parents were staying with us, Robert only wanted my help most of the time. Because I was getting interrupted sleep at night, it was hard to concentrate some days. When I got home from work, and after Robert went to bed, I would catch up on emails etc, before the nightly routine of Robert's pain would start. Robert's doctor tried several different medications over a two-week period to try and ease the pain, but nothing was working.

It all came to a head in late March. By now, Robert's acute pain attacks were occurring every night, every two hours and he was taking a mix of pain drugs that I knew was well above the safe directions of use. In one weekend Robert took up to 18 Panamax in a day. Over that weekend he nearly took 40 Panamax to get through the weekend. I was so worried; we were fighting a lot. We both hadn't slept much, we were both crying a lot, and I was at my wits end. So, on the Sunday night, after recording everything I had given to Robert for the pain, I emailed his doctor outlining the regime.

Thankfully, because I sent that email, Robert's doctor referred him to a highly recommended palliative care or pain doctor that week. In the meantime, we were given advice of a safer dosage regime to ensure it did not kill him.

Pressure and Pain

When we saw the pain doctor that week, he told us of a case that had occurred the previous week where a patient had overdosed on Panadol, which, if taken incorrectly, and especially if consuming more than 8 tablets per day over a certain period, causes your organs to deteriorate and fail. Robert was so lucky that it had not happened to him and after fighting this horrible disease, it was so terrible to think that he could have overdosed. Although the fights between Robert and I were emotional and draining over the previous weekend, I was grateful that I had reacted and emailed his doctor. I could not bear to think what may have happened if I hadn't.

The pain doctor gave Robert a new regime, prescribing medications that only he could. They were high dose, but after a few days Robert would start to see the pain subside and hopefully not as often. So, within 10 minutes after putting these medications under his tongue the pain would subside. The important thing was to try and catch it quickly so that it did not rise to above six out of ten. The aim was to keep the pain at around four to five and then the medications, once at the right dosage, would take it down to two.

All I wanted was to have my husband pain-free. I knew that was a steep ask, but right now he was not moving out of the house, only moving between the lounge room and bathroom and even then, I had to walk with him in case he lost his balance. Robert was also not drinking or eating enough, and his weight was now down to 70 kilograms. I was trying hard to cook or buy food that tasted good as the nutritional value at this stage did not matter.

Robert also was not talking much. When Robert is scared or worried, he would shut down. Even trying to watch TV was an effort for him. He was very distracted by what he was physically feeling and I could have only imagined what he was thinking.

After seeing the pain doctor on the Thursday, I then had my three best friends coming to visit on the Friday. These three girls have always been there for me. My best friend, Meagan, of 43 years; my girlfriend, Colleen, who is Robert's best mate's wife, we had been friends for 21 years; and my third friend, Denise, who I have known through Colleen for 19 years. The four of us call ourselves 'The Alphas'. We have supported each other through thick and thin and had developed a great foursome friendship over the last few years. After the last couple of weeks, I needed my girlfriends more than ever and it was such a relief to see them.

Robert was not up to much conversation when they arrived on the Friday night, but he did the best he could. The girls were so happy to be there and although Robert would normally have sat and chatted, he was struggling with the conversation. He sat with us for dinner, which was particularly unusual. He was trying so hard to be normal, but the pain on his face told a different story. He went to bed early as he was in so much pain. He was apologising to me when I was helping him into bed because he just could not sit due to the pain. I just wished he would take the pain meds earlier to help himself.

When I returned to the girls a short time later, they all commented on how much Robert had changed. He was thinner, very distracted, and they could all see the pain in his face. It was good for me to hear that they could see the change, but they were more worried about me. How was I coping, how was I balancing everything, getting through? I gave them a response, but I know I was not being completely honest. Honesty would've meant letting the emotion spill out, and I certainly could not afford to do that at this stage. I was holding it together, being strong for the both of us, but I could feel that breaking point was coming - and fast.

That Sunday was the worst I had seen Robert. He was now drinking even less fluids, his food intake was the size of a toddler's and he spent the whole day in our bedroom. Denise went in to see him and sat on the bed. I do not know what they talked about, but Denise felt the need to chat to Robert. She is especially grateful for that chat now, because at the time she did not know it, but two months later she would come to know that this would be her last conversation with Robert. Sunday night was much the same, with continual pain attacks that were not as bad as the ones a week ago but were still occurring with regularity, which meant interrupted sleep.

On Monday morning, I was taking the girls to the airport and then Robert and I were going to the clinic. I had taken the day off work, so all I had to be concerned about was the girls and Robert. As we drove to the airport Robert did not say a word. Looking at him I knew something serious was up, although as usual he was not telling me. We dropped the girls off and they were concerned as well. But we were going to the clinic so at least the nurses could address what was going on.

We had got halfway to Brisbane when Robert asked me to pull off the highway, he needed food as he felt nauseas. During this period Robert was a MacDonald's addict. I say that tongue in cheek, but MacDonald's was one of those foods that he could keep down and it tasted good to him. Of course, where I pulled off, they didn't have a McDonald's so the only thing I could do was get him to the clinic quickly.

I did not speed that morning, but in my head, I wanted to be a jet airplane. I could've pulled over and rang an ambulance, but I needed to get Robert to the clinic. He trusted the nurses and we would've had a fight if I made that decision and I just didn't want to incite any anger between us. The drive was the worst drive ever. I felt sick and could not get him there quick enough.

Once I got Robert inside, his favourite nurse came to meet us. I had messaged her saying Robert was in a bad way. When she saw him, she immediately took him down the back to his chair and started to ask him questions. It only took a minute before she looked at me. I had tears in my eyes, and she indicated for me to follow her down the hall. I was not even halfway down the hall when I burst into tears.

She took me into a room and I just lost it. I was so worried about Robert, I had not seen him like this, he was not coherent, he was distant and would not tell me what was really going on. She comforted me, hugging me, and saying it will be ok. We will ring Robert's doctor and he will know what to do. But I told her I must have him admitted to hospital, that I did not care which hospital, but I was not taking him home. Robert was extremely ill, which the nurses could see and it was beyond my own caring and nursing skills now. He had to go to hospital he needed urgent care.

The nurse held me tight for what seemed like a few minutes, helping me to release all this burden. Once I started crying, the tears just would not stop. But I did feel a level of weight lift off my shoulders that I had been carrying around for weeks. Trying to do the right thing for Robert, working, running the house, 35 acres and being a hostess to my friends had slapped me in the face, and it was now all being released down my cheeks.

The nurse told me that she did not need convincing that Robert needed to go to hospital, she could see it and his blood results confirmed it. His haemoglobin (red blood cells) was low, his platelets were low and now he had a nosebleed as a result of his platelets. After two bags of platelets, red blood and a lot of fluid, I took Robert to the hospital where he was admitted.

During the day, I also made that same round of phone calls. Crying during each one, I repeated the same story over and over again: "Robert's extremely sick, he needs to be admitted, I will keep you updated." I rang my boss, after organising someone to stand in for me, and told him I would be taking at least the next few days off until I worked out what was going on. Work was so supportive telling me you just be with Robert and we will worry about everything else here. I did not have to be told that, I wasn't worrying about anything else other than Robert right now, but it was comforting to know that this company and who ever I worked for always supported me in putting Robert's health first.

Robert was admitted to the palliative care ward at the hospital. Not because he was a palliative care candidate but because his palliative care/pain management doctor was the head of that ward and would team up with Robert's doctor to administer whatever treatment Robert needed. It was a bit daunting being in such a ward. This is where people came to die, I had to get my head around that that was not the fact for Robert, and I had to keep telling myself why he was here.

2019 had not begun the way that Robert or I had wanted. The pressure on both of us was extreme. Our ability to manage ourselves was not working and we needed assistance to work through it. For all the times that I had cared for Robert this time was different. I felt that Robert was not telling me what he was really thinking and maybe that was because for the first real time, he was scared too.

Chapter 10

The Dress Rehearsal

Fifteen hours after Robert was admitted to hospital, the first of many events occurred. I was sitting with Robert and he started to feel unwell. The nurse came and found that his heart rate was 160. A normal heart rate sits around 80-100, resting less. Robert's had been up around 100 for a month or so and it was put down to the medications. But the protocol in the hospitals is anything over 150 meant calling the the Medical Emergency Response Team (MERT).

The MERT are from the Intensive Care Unit (ICU). They specialise in acute care, especially when it comes to things around the heart. They administered more fluid and a liquid called Albumin, which assists in bringing the heart rate down. I was not too concerned; I had seen this before and Robert's blood pressure was good. At the time of this incident Robert was wanting to know what all the fuss was about.

There was a crew of six doctors and nurses in the room and he could not understand why. Typical Robert playing it down.

The ICU doctor pulled me aside and wanted to talk to me alone. She started to tell me that as Robert is a relapse Leukaemia patient that they needed to know whether Robert would want to be taken to the ICU. If Robert's heart starts to fail and he was up in the ward the doctors could only put him on a respirator with limited procedures and that he might die. She had spoken to Robert's doctor and she was aware that Robert's wishes were not to be taken to ICU. I told her I knew this but wanted to know why we were talking about dying. Who said Robert is going to die? I then proceeded to tell her that Robert is in the palliative care ward due to the pain treatment not because it's the end of his life.

I was in shock. I could not believe what was being said to me. There must have been some mistake. Why has Robert's doctor not told me this? All I could think was that Robert's doctor had not told us the truth, that Robert was here because he was dying.

The confronting questions did not stop. I was then asked what Robert's wishes were. I didn't know, we hadn't discussed it. All I could think of was why are we discussing this now, this is so confusing, I just didn't get it. My head was filled with so many questions and I just didn't understand what was going on.

It took around an hour for Robert's vital signs to return to normal. He was so determined that he wasn't going to die, so I didn't understand why all of these people had jumped to that conclusion. I had to speak to Robert's doctor and understand what was going on.

On this day I also met two of the pain doctors that worked on the ward. One sat down with us and explained what had happened and what they were there to do. The nurses had taken blood cultures to see if there was an infection present and Robert had an X-ray and ultrasound of his liver to see if that was causing the reaction. Thankfully, both of those came back clear. Robert's liver was good, but he did have an E. coli infection which would be treated with antibiotics.

We were then able to speak to Robert's doctor and the nurses and doctors had reacted as expected. He told me not to worry that Robert wasn't here because he was dying, it was because of the pain and in this ward, Robert had the best of the best in doctor care. Well, that was a relief. I didn't understand what all the fuss was about, but thankfully we now had some answers. He also told Robert that he would be in hospital for at least a week and that he needed to try and put some weight on!

Over the next few days, it seemed that as soon as the doctors got one thing under control another would pop up. He was now getting fevers, temperatures of over 38 a couple of times a day due to the infection and it would take a few days for the antibiotics to start working. Over these initial days we also had visits from the chaplain, counsellor, a not for profit organisation called Dreams2live and the infectious disease doctors. At one stage it was like a revolving door. All of them had something different to tell me in which I would take notes and there seemed to always be something new for me to investigate online. Days like these were exhausting and felt like nothing was going in the right direction.

In the first week, I took advantage of talking to the counsellor, chaplain, and pain doctor. They were great at giving me the ability to talk about Robert by myself and were all quite concerned with how I was feeling. I needed that as even though I was talking to family and friends regularly, these services were different. They would ask me questions that would also release the burden I felt inside me, and I always felt better for it post their chats.

Over the first weekend that Robert was in hospital he had a second episode which was identified as a second infection. The fevers were now more frequent, and Robert was now hallucinating from the pain medication. The infectious disease doctor increased Robert's antibiotic regime to try and kill the infection.

My level of concern was heightened but I could still see Robert showing a level of fight by getting out of bed to go to the toilet and showering. This is what I needed to see. Small levels of fight in him otherwise I would have started to give up.

After a week of being in hospital and with no discharge in sight, Robert's symptoms were unchanged. Robert's pain was being managed now but he was still having episodes of delirium. On one of the days, Robert was patting the bed. He told me the dogs were on the bed with him and he was talking to them. Having seen it all before, I went with the flow, acknowledging Robert when he spoke to me about the dogs and encouraged him to believe that it was real. I had learnt previously not to question his visions as it would just make him frustrated and angry.

During the next week I spoke to the counsellor and pain management doctor about Robert's progress. They started to prepare me for the worst. They told me that if we didn't start to see some positive signs soon, then maybe Robert's body would start giving up.

This wasn't something I wanted to think about, but they were right, I could not block this out as a possibility. They wanted to make sure that I was giving a level of reality to our families in Melbourne so that it did not come out of left field and they felt like I had not been keeping them informed of the truth. As much as I wanted to protect them by giving them an optimistic view of the situation, there was also the reality that this might not end the way we all hoped.

This advice was priceless. They helped me to word my sentences to ensure everyone understood what was happening, but also told me not to sugar coat the situation. They would always follow up with me the next day to understand how the calls went and if I had any concerns or questions would continue to help me through them. I always felt much better going into the calls after this preparation and was so grateful for their care towards me.

Since coming down to Brisbane, I had been staying at a friend's house, Kyran and Mitch's, so that I didn't have to make the two-hour drive up and down the highway every day. I met Mitch through work in Brisbane and as soon as I met Kyran I knew we were destined to be great friends. She has a fun-loving nature and is straight up. She has such a warm caring personality and we just clicked from the start. I remember the call on the Monday saying I need somewhere to stay can I come to your place.

It was nice coming back to their house as I could debrief on the day's events, have a small piece of normality with them before retiring for the night to do it all again tomorrow. They didn't disturb me when I was sleeping, their three kids were awesome always happy and including me in their days' goings-on. Their youngest daughter even let me have her room while she slept in her sister's bed. It was so good to be around caring, loving, beautiful people, and it took a level of stress out of my exhausting days.

On Good Friday, I started to see some signs of Robert going downhill. He didn't eat much, didn't get out of bed and he was very delirious. So many holidays or celebrations over the last five years had been pushed aside or missed due to Robert's illness and on this day, I wanted to have a little bit of down time for myself. So I did not let the signals get to me, I pushed it aside and left the hospital a little earlier so that I could go back to Kyran and Mitch's where I was cooking for them that night.

It was also good for me to have a little bit of extra time away from the hospital. It had been 12 days since Robert was admitted and the daily routine was taking its toll. I was inside Robert's room for 8 to 12 hours a day. The rooms were freezing cold due to the air conditioning and when you are in a palliative care ward every day you see things that make your heart break.

Every few days, I would see someone losing a loved one and you work out the routine when someone on the ward dies. The nurses usually shut everyone's doors and you hear or see the long steel box being taken down the hallway. It was always a reminder that life can be cut short at the blink of an eye, and you continually see the grief and sadness from other families on this ward.

My relaxing night with our friends was swept away the next day. On Saturday, I saw a vastly different Robert. He didn't eat at all, his delirium was at an all-time high, and I just didn't feel good about this. I made the usual enquiries with the nurses about what the doctors had said, but none of it was good. Robert didn't know where he was, so I made the decision to ring our friends, John and Di. I didn't want to alert the family yet, but I needed someone by my side as this was all getting really scary.

Then, the reality of the moment struck that afternoon. While sitting next to Robert with John, Robert, out of the blue asked me if "he was dying". I instantly felt the tears rolling down my face as my worst nightmare may now be my reality. I replied back to him, saying, "That only you know if you're dying". Then he responded with the most heartbreaking response, "Yeah I think I am dying." I left the room with John and just started to sob uncontrollably. This was it, I was going to lose Robert. This wasn't supposed to happen, he was supposed to keep fighting. But I had also seen for myself what his mind and body had been through and it was now taking its biggest toll.

After pulling myself together, I asked the nurse to contact the weekend doctor. After examining Robert, he told me that he was deteriorating. He also told me what would start to happen if his body was giving up. In the meantime, he gave Robert some additional medication and said they would watch him closely and keep me updated.

With the comfort of John and Di beside me, I started to make those heartbreaking calls. Firstly, to my mum and dad and brother, then to Robert's parents, brother and sister. After telling them what had happened that day, I basically said if you want to see Robert before he possibly dies than you better arrange a flight asap because I don't know how much time he has. It was so damn hard. I even remember saying to Robert's mum after she asked me are you sure, I yelled down the phone with such emotion saying, "Your son is dying".

I felt so bad saying that after I said it, but they had to know the reality even though they had always been positive and optimistic. Now was not the time to think that he was going to fight, I just needed them to come to Brisbane so that if this was the time, they had no regrets by not saying goodbye.

Everyone reacted quickly and within 30 minutes of making those calls, my parents, Robert's parents, sister and brother had all booked flights. They were all coming to Brisbane on the first available flights out of Melbourne and would all be with me by tomorrow.

To accommodate the family and enable me to stay with Robert, he had been moved to a larger room. As each family member arrived, I took them to Robert and by this time he was unresponsive. The team were still administering the antibiotics and medications but had stopped giving him blood products.

Everyone was so distressed, especially Robert's parents. They sat by his side praying and begging him to recover, begging him to come back to us, that it wasn't his time, and it was too soon. Robert's dad is an extremely emotional man and was sobbing so hard, saying no son, no son. While his mother is a strong woman and was telling his dad to stop crying you must be strong. You must be strong for Bobby if you can't stop crying you have to leave. His emotions were raw, while Robert's mother's were a signal that the family had to be brave, courageous, and not be negative. It was so hard to watch, it was breaking my heart and I could not imagine how they were feeling seeing their son like this.

While they were saying these things, I was doing the opposite. I was saying if this is your time and you can see the angels, then spread your own wings and I am ok if you need to go. Of course, I wasn't ok for him to go, but after everything he had gone through, I couldn't beg him to stay. For me it felt so selfish to ask Robert to keep going because of my pain, because I did not want to be by myself, because I could not live life without him.

At around midnight on Easter Saturday, the bedside vigil started. While I stayed in Robert's room, Robert's parents stayed at the hospital and Robert's brother and sister stayed at a hotel across the road.

When my parents arrived the following day, I jumped into their arms and could not stop crying. Robert was a second son to my parents, and they had seen the worst days, especially over March when they were staying at our house. They knew that Robert had possibly reached his limits and if it was his time for him to go, then he should go.

My mum is a strong woman. She barely showed her emotions during these times. She is like me, strong until you don't have to be strong, and a mess after that. Whereas my dad wears his heart on his sleeve.

The Dress Rehearsal

Over the years, he had had so many amazing times with his son-in-law and although he was heartbroken, he told his son-in-law that if it was time to go he must go.

I was also grateful that John and Di came back to the hospital the next day. John is a great friend and in this situation was focusing on me and was with me whenever I spoke to the doctors. When the doctor told me the medication that he gave Robert the day before wasn't working and then asked if I would like to stop the antibiotics, John and I would discuss the options of what this would mean. That wasn't from a medical perspective, but from my family and my own expectations.

At that point there was still a small part of me that had some hope, so I told the doctor no. I couldn't stop his treatment at this point for a number of reasons and thankfully after explaining them to the doctor he understood. He told me he would give it another 24 hours and we would discuss it again tomorrow.

During this time, I also talked to John about Robert's burial wishes. I knew he wanted to be buried, we had had that conversation many years ago but what we hadn't discussed was where. We had lived in Brisbane for nearly ten years, but we didn't have a resting place here. The reality was that I was only 46 and what if I moved away from Queensland at some point. I didn't want Robert to be in some cemetery that no one visited. I also thought that if anyone needed to visit Robert more than I did it would be his parents. So, I made the decision to take him back to Melbourne. I knew burying Robert in Melbourne was the right thing to do. I needed John to know this in case further arrangements needed to be made and if I could not do it, I would ask John to help.

Throughout Easter Sunday night, there was no change in Robert. He wasn't conscious, his breathing was deep and had taken on a rattle. I had heard that rattle before when I visited my grandpa when he was dying. Robert was breathing so hard and his throat was so dry that his breathing was very distressed. Family and friends continued to sit by his side reminiscing about good times, childhood memories, or just giving him their thoughts.

All our family and friends had now been informed of Robert's condition and everyone's heart was breaking. They knew the love, bond and relationship Robert and I had. They would refer to us as Team Gomes as we did everything together. I knew there were silent thoughts, prayers and conversations happening throughout Australia and the world as he was loved by so many people.

Overnight, a miracle happened. I found a quote which I posted on Robert's private Facebook group that said, "When the world says give up, Hope whispers try it one more time" from Dr Michelle Bengtson. That is what Robert did. In the early hours of Monday morning Robert woke up. Robert had responded to the medications; Robert wasn't going to die! Maybe those pearly gates weren't about to open for him yet. Maybe it wasn't his time and he just needed to scare the living life out of us.

All I knew is that I couldn't love this man more than I did that morning. I was so relieved and thought maybe he just had to go the depths of doom to then restart his fight again.

Everyone was so overwhelmed with emotion. The day was filled with smiles and laughter. Robert's parents were relieved that they hadn't lost their eldest son. It had been a traumatic two days for them and I will never know what it feels like to sit by your sons' side when he is dying. It doesn't matter whether your child is one, 18 or 47, a parent should not have to go through this. Thankfully their prayers had been answered and they had a second chance with their son.

The Dress Rehearsal

Although there was a lot of joy in the room, after speaking to the doctors I was still being quite cautious. I had heard of people coming back from a near death experience only to die in the coming day. Even though I told Robert how much I loved him, how proud of him I was, that I would be by his side for as long as he needed me, that we would do this together, I still wasn't letting my guard down. I still felt unsettled and needed to protect my heart.

His sister made the decision to go home that afternoon. She was exhausted and had three girls under five waiting for her. This had taken a huge toll on her, which yes it did on everyone, but Robert's sister and he are close. They mightn't talk a lot but her face lights up when she is with her brother. I never realised this to the extent I did until I saw her over these two days. Her raw emotion, distress and sadness was nothing that I had seen before. I felt for her because I know what a love for your brother was like and I would be the same if it was my brother.

For the next few days, Robert started to eat more and more. He was able to sit up on the side of the bed which was great progress and he was able to have conversations with his parents and brother. It was a special time for everyone, but it was exhausting as well. A few people came to visit Robert, but I did not want too many people around while his family was there. I wanted this to be their time.

When Robert's parents made the decision to leave on the Thursday, they were so happy. There were now tears of happiness that had replaced the tears of sadness. They knew their son had a long way to go, but they were happy to see the progress in the last few days and knew with Robert's fight he would be home soon.

The hugs they gave me and the words that were spoken that day formed a bond between us that I had not felt in years. Yes, we had become a lot closer when they came to care for Robert at our house in 2015, but this was different. They had seen again how much I cared for Robert, loved Robert and would be by his side always. This gave them so much happiness and hope that through our love, Robert would survive and go into remission.

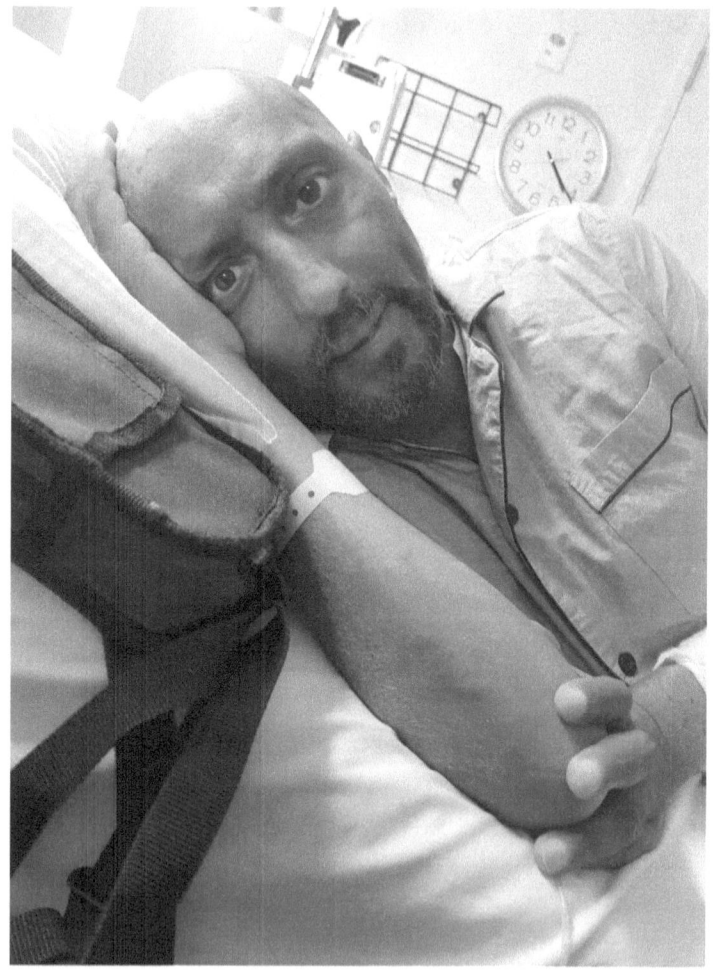

Robert's brother also left on the Thursday. He had left his wife, Kim, and their four kids in Sydney when I made the call on the Saturday as they had been holidaying there. With Robert out of the woods he could spend a few more days with them before travelling home.

Robert's brother is a quiet man. He does not say much and holds his emotions close to him. He is a thinker and most of the time I did not know what he was thinking, but I knew he loved his brother so much. Robert was Jason's older brother, was always someone he looked up to and I could see that this week had taken a lot out of him. I knew his kids would give him big hugs when he saw them that night and they would help heal him.

Then there were mum, dad and I. My parents had been staying nearby at accommodation that was mostly used by families of cancer patients that were having long term treatment at the hospital. On Saturday, they were returning to my place and I was going back to stay with Kyran and Mitch. Although all of us were still a little uncertain with how long it would take Robert to improve enough to come home, my friends were more than happy to have me at their house for however long it took, and mum and dad were happy to be up the farm to look after our property.

Chapter 11

The Rollercoaster Ride

After the scare over Easter and the improvement Robert had shown, they moved him to another room. It was now time to go back to the daily hospital routine and for Robert to start his recovery.

The daily routine reverted back to what I was doing previously, including staying at Kyran and Mitch's again. I would get into the hospital before lunch and we would have lunch together. I would then help Robert shower and sit with him until after dinner.

Showering Robert was not something that worried me. We had a routine and he felt so much more comfortable with me doing it. At this point Robert had lost a lot of weight and was under 60 kilograms, so helping him walk into the bathroom and move in the shower was not difficult either.

When I was not helping Robert, we had the TV on and I would read a book. I had a few books of my own and I borrowed a few from Kyran. During this time, the books I needed to read just jumped out at me. I enjoyed the stories, but their messages especially resonated with me and what I was going through emotionally.

Robert did not have many visitors during this time. The only weekly visitors were my parents, John and Di, and his blood brothers Rob and Claire and Heinke and Richard. If I went down to the café with them, I would talk about my frustration and sadness. That I did not see Robert progressing and maybe he was losing the fight. Everyone would agree, but when Robert keeps telling you he is not giving up, then you know he is not. Just hearing that from these friends would be enough for me to go back up, sit and be hopeful that one day I would walk in and he would have turned the page.

On the evening of the 29th of April, I was becoming more and more worried about Robert's emotional state. I was worried that much that I decided to write a letter to him because I could not tell him verbally.

Dear Robert

I wanted to write this because I cannot get the words together to say it to you.

I will never know what you go through, how you get through it and what your days really feel like. It is so easy for me at times to say things to either push you along, give you hope or give you another perspective. I want you to know that I only do it as I love you, care for you and just want the very best for you.

I do want you to know that I am very worried about you right now. What I see when sitting with you each day is that you are eating less most days, your losing weight, your ability to motivate yourself to start to move away from the bed is very limited and I just feel you are going backwards.

For me watching this after all the days, weeks, months and years of fighting makes me so sad I know that you have had the roughest time possible, but seeing you not doing the basic things really upsets me. I don't know whether you are scared, your tired, you are worried at what life is going to be, but whatever it is I am here to support you, to help and care for you.

I want you to be able to come home, to be able to play with the dogs, even if it is from a seat, and to be able to have a level of independence that allows you to continually improve. But right now, I feel that your ability to be able to reach those milestones will be limited by the steps you are currently doing in the hospital. I want you to be able to have your next round of chemo, the DLI from a point that does not cause you to be in hospital for long periods again. I want you to be able to go to the bathroom by yourself, walk to the kitchen to get something out of the fridge, just generally have a life that is fulfilling.

But right now, without small steps being achieved each day, I just cannot see you getting there. This is not like other times your starting point is well behind those. I so want you to go home, for me to go home, because I do not like living away from home either. I just cannot see that happening. Our home is not equipped for supporting you right now. But if you feel that how you are today is what you will be forever then we have other decisions to make.

Please understand that everything I am saying, wanting to see you do, is to enable you to live with a quality of life that is more than just a lounge and a bed. I love you so much that I only ever want the best for you, but when I see you wanting to gradually get back to that sort of life, it is so sad, stressful and keeps me awake at night.

I love you heaps, and never want to fight with you, and if I am not supporting you in the way you need then tell me, but my intention is to never lose you, just help you to achieve your best life.

I will never give up on you, even if you give up on yourself, my love for you is too strong to not want the best for you, for me, for us.

Xxxxxxxx"

I remember writing this letter in bed whilst crying, thinking about when the best time would be to read it to him. But when I arrived the following day, it was like he had read it. He asked to get the physiotherapist in, started to drink more fluids and seemed like he had his fight back. I did not give him the letter and instead kept it on my iPad for myself.

For Robert, his day was trying to manage his pain through the cocktail of break through drugs that were available to him, managing small fevers and working with the physiotherapist.

In the week of the 29th of April, he was eager to do the exercises outside of the formal sessions. He was starting to eat more and had increased his weight from 58 kilograms to 62 kilograms. His energy and drive were improving, and it made the days more pleasurable for me.

But with every step forward there seems to be one backward and this time it was the delirium. Out of everything Robert went through, in terms of symptoms or reactions to the drugs over the six years, the delirium was the scariest to watch. Robert would start to slur his words, mumble and when I would ask him if he was ok, he would turn his head, look at me with his eyes wide open and say "what?" I knew he did not know what he was doing, saying and typically me asking him this would just annoy him.

When the hallucinations took a turn for the worst it was on the night of the 4th of May. Mum and dad always visited Robert on a Sunday and were already there when I arrived. As I came into the room Robert started to explain the trauma he had experienced the night before.

He had thought that someone had come into his room and told him there was a bomb in there. He started to shout out to the nurses saying there is a bomb in here, you must ring Suzanne, you must evacuate the patients, we are all going to die. When they tried to calm him down, he started to cry uncontrollably saying, "Ring Suzanne, ring Suzanne, you must tell her." They ended up giving Robert a sedative to calm him down, but even when he was retelling the story, he was still quite emotional. I could only imagine what the nurses experienced with him that night and what memories he had in his head now.

On the following night, the nurses had a similar event and it seemed that the hallucinations would happen at night after his methadone dosage. The methadone was administered to Robert to eliminate his pain, but was now affecting his brain. The following day he was sent for an MRI and the head of the palliative care ward and the pain doctor came to see us with the results.

What they had seen was that Robert's brain looked a bit yucky. In other words, your brain is supposed to have a layer of fluid between the brain the layer that keeps it all in tack. When they saw Robert's, that layer was hugging the brain like meat in a cryovac.

The doctor explained that there were two possibilities here. Either there is an infection in the brain or Robert may have secondary brain cancer. But in the meantime, we will treat it as an infection and see if that improves his situation. They also decided to take him off the methadone to see if that would eliminate the hallucinations. The news of secondary brain cancer concerned me and I did not want to think that was even possible. Robert did not seem to react to that news and we never talked about it being a possibility.

The following day things started to continue to go downhill. Robert's heart rate went above 150 beats a minute, the ICU doctors were called, I had another conversation with them saying if the drugs that were being administered did not take the heart rate down then I had to make the decision of whether he would go to Intensive care or not which limited the treatment they would give him. I had already had the discussion with Robert a couple of weeks before and he told me he did not want to go to ICU, so I gave the doctor the decision immediately.

The doctor then asked me if Robert had a heart attack, would I want them to administer CPR. I also said no as Robert had also told me that he did not want to be resuscitated either. This was the third time I had had this conversation in the last month and although it was not as daunting as the first, and Robert and I had discussed the options, it was still a discussion that I did not like having. Again, after administering the drugs Robert's heart rate dropped and he was again asking what all the fuss was about.

The following day, which Robert had been in hospital for 32 days, Robert's doctor recommended that to increase Robert's weight, that I needed to bring MacDonald's in for lunch. So, I did what the doctor ordered and even though I took a picture to send to our family and friends of Robert eating it, he ate about half and said he was full. All

I could think of was that if he couldn't eat McDonald's then what would he eat, and how would be put on enough weight for him to come home?

By now I was starting to struggle, and it was now time to seek further counselling by the hospital's chaplain. As a child I never really understood my faith. I was christened Presbyterian, same as my mother. I went to Sunday School, which I think was convenient for mum and dad to get me out of the house on a Sunday morning, or it was because my mum was a Sunday School teacher in her youth. I also sometimes went to church with my best friend Meagan and her mum on Sunday nights. Those Sunday night sessions were a time where I could spend more time with Meagan and we would run around the grounds of the church.

Even when Robert and I were planning our service for our wedding, a church never came into it. Robert and his family were Catholic, but Robert did not want to get married in a church. He never practised his religion, and with me not being religious, he did not see that it was necessary that we got married in a church.

But when Robert was diagnosed, the first night I was alone in bed by myself, I decided that I needed to do whatever was possible to bring the powers that were in the universe to my husband to help him fight this terrible disease. So, from time to time, I would look up to the sky, and start talking out loud to whoever was listening. To ask them to be with Robert and help him along this road he had been made to take.

The hospital Robert was in was run by the Uniting Church and they had chaplains and a chapel for those who wanted to access their services. Since meeting the chaplain I really liked her and we had been having regular chats on the ward. She was easy to talk to and she cared about my wellbeing.

I talked to her about Robert's struggles and their effect on me. That for me, I was making sure I got enough sleep, did not overindulge with alcohol, and just tried to be there for Robert without losing my mental state. What we focused on the most was how I was communicating to our families. Most of this conversation was centred around bad news. How I was coping with the conversations with the doctors, how I was conveying that to the family and what else could she help me with.

These conversations, and learning how to cope with the worst, were uncomfortable to sit through. There was no talk of faith, of joining a service or a church, and there was no pressure to read the Bible or its verses. It was genuine support and care for my wellbeing and how I was coping with the everyday life of being a carer, of sitting with Robert for hours on end and dealing with this rollercoaster ride.

But while I was downstairs with the chaplain, another event had happened with Robert. As I got up from the table, I noticed that I had multiple missed calls from the ward. After rushing back up there I found out that Robert had had a hallucination and during it he recalled the doctor saying that they were considering taking the 'picc line' in his arm out, through which all of his medication was administered. Robert decided that he would pull it out himself. He pulled it and panicked, but instead of calling the nurses he put it on the table and put pressure on his arm, like the nurses do. Thank god that he did have some sense of reality and knew what the procedure of removing was and he was able to stem the blood flow.

Thankfully, a nurse came in and Robert did not sustain any other injuries. But it scared both Robert and I as the hallucinations were taking on a whole new level of risk.

To also ensure Robert was safe at all times, they moved Robert to a room outside the nurses station and engaged a security man that would sit in Robert's room 24/7 until the doctors and the nurses felt that Robert was not at risk in harming himself. Having someone in the room ready to call the nurses if there was any danger was not something I had ever expected.

At this point Robert had become quite childlike. He was now asking the nurses or myself if things were right or wrong, things that an adult would automatically do. Whether he could eat this or that. He was making comments that did not make sense and at times he did not even know who I was. He was not the man I used to know, and I just had to dig deep down in the depths of my beliefs that it was possible for him to regain part of his former self. I went to bed that night after downloading to Kyran and Mitch, hoping some relief would come over the following days. Every day was so distressing, and I hated seeing Robert like this.

Over the next few days, which had now been 36 days in hospital, there were some glimmers of hope. It was either McDonald's or Hungry Jack's for lunch and Robert would do his best every day to eat as much as he could. He was walking between the bed and the bathroom with his intravenous pole and he was completing his physiotherapy sessions every day. He was now sitting up in the recliner in his room for around five hours a day, something he had not done for weeks.

I was so proud of him and it gave me the much-needed confidence that Robert would be released from hospital. The icing on the cake was when Robert told his doctor that he would be ready to go home by the end of the week and then do clinic visits the following week. I was blown away and I had never seen him be this committed for weeks.

Over that week, he really ramped up the physiotherapist sessions. He was able to walk around the ward with his walker, even though it was a challenge he was doing it. He was eating everything he could and if he were in any pain beyond what was bearable, he would manage it with the nurses and ask for the pain medications.

On day 40 after receiving his blood products, with a truck load of medications, it was time to go home. I never thought this day would come, neither did Robert. We could not wipe the smiles off our faces and I could not wait to finally lie next to my husband in bed again.

When we got in the car and before driving out of the hospital, Robert was crying. He said to me, "I did not think I was going to make it out". I said to him, "Neither did I a couple of times. But you are, so sit back and enjoy the ride." As we drove back to our home two hours from the hospital, I recalled the multiple times that I thought I would only ever do this drive alone. As the silent tears slid down my face, I realised they were tears of joy that Robert had fought and made it. If there was any place that Robert would fully recover it was home!

Our parents with Robert and I at Robert's surprise party March 2018

Chapter 12

Hope Turns to Heartache

My parents were so happy to see us drive up to the house and have Robert home. Again, the tears flowed from Robert when he saw his puppies and hugged my mum and dad. I didn't know whether Robert was ready to go home, but his doctor always said that being at home is the best place to recover and I know he would not have let Robert come home if there was any risk.

On our first night home Robert was exhausted from the drive. It had been an emotional day and the feeling for him to be sleeping in his own bed was something he had yearned for 42 days. For me, I just wanted him to know that I was by his side and I never wanted him to go through the events of the last 42 days again.

My love for Robert had grown even more as a result of his immense strength and determination, more than I ever thought it could, and

I would do whatever was needed to set up our home to make it comfortable for him. When I got into bed he kissed and hugged me, and said, "Thank you for all you have done, and I love you so much". I didn't need Robert to tell me that to keep being by his side, but I did feel so much love for this man right now, hearing that today meant so much.

The weekend was exceptionally low-key. Heinke and Richard came over with scones and jam and a box of chocolates for Robert to celebrate his return home. It was nice to see them so happy, especially Richard seeing he had had a transplant too. The day that Richard came to the hospital and said his goodbye to Robert, thinking he was never going to see him again, I imagined it was like his own life flashing in front of him. It was a moment that I never wanted to see again and to see Richard full of life on this day made me so happy.

I do however remember breakfast on the Sunday morning. Like we always did, Robert asked for eggs. He loved his eggs, and fresh ones from our chooks made him so happy. So, I made eggs for us and my parents. The dogs were with us and we all sat outside chatting and enjoying the view. I do remember looking at Robert and watching him staring into the distance. I did not know what he was thinking but I'm sure he thought he would never see those mountains again. Although knowing what I do today, it was one of Robert's wishes early on that if he died, he wanted to die at home. Maybe on this day he was taking in that view for the very last time. Who knew. All I know is that it bought a smile to my face and I wanted to cherish this moment for the rest of our lives.

For the next few weeks, we would have to live down in Brisbane on weekdays as Robert would need to visit the cancer clinic three times a week for monitoring and treatment. It was a better option than hospital, but it did put a lot more pressure and work on me. When I say this, I never want everyone to feel that I was ungrateful for having to do this, it was the complete opposite, but being the carer 24/7 was going to be a lot more difficult this time.

The one thing that continued to frustrate me was when Robert was not eating to the level the doctors wanted him to. I made a special effort to make sure he had his favourite foods. We would buy McDonald's for lunch every day, I would buy Robert donuts, croissants, chips, ice cream, and make him curry for dinner. But his appetite seemed to continue to reduce and I could see it was such an effort for him to force himself to eat every meal.

On the Friday of the first week in Brisbane, we had his last clinic appointment before heading home. His weight was at 60 kilograms, which was one kilogram more than when he left hospital. His blood numbers were good and there were no leukaemia cells. These were all good signs and I went into the weekend with some confidence that things were heading in the right direction.

As soon as we arrived home, Robert started to get anxious about walking from the car, about going to the bathroom, about being anywhere in the house but our bedroom. What had happened on the way home, what had caused this? All his meals over that weekend were given to him in bed and he hardly had any energy to talk. The devil in my head was telling me that this might be closer to the end than I thought. But the angel was saying its ok, don't over think this, it's just a small backward step, nothing to worry about.

But when I stopped by the door and watched Robert laying in the bed looking out of our bedroom window to those hills it scared me. He wasn't moving, wasn't talking and didn't even know I was standing there. Through the remainder of the weekend, the hallucinations began to come back, his eyes were cloudy, and I really could not wait to get him back to the clinic on Monday for the nurses to check him out.

I told my parents that I was worried and that I might have to ask for him to be admitted to hospital again. They could see that things were going backwards and reassured me that whatever I had to do for Robert that I had their support. That meant so much as I knew getting him admitted again was going to be a fight that I may have to have.

As we pulled up at the clinic on Monday and I lifted Robert out of the car and he sat on the walker's chair, he looked deflated and old. He was not able to walk with the support of the walker and I was grateful when we saw a friend who is a physiotherapist at the clinic as I knew she may be able to motivate him to start moving again. She was able to give him an exercise regime that was done on the bed or a couch and for the first night Robert did them a few times which gave me hope.

On Tuesday, however, the delirium worsened. While we were sitting on the couch, he told me his mum was in the room. He was talking to the television like there were actual people in the room and he had no sense of where he was. The delirium continued through the night and he woke up several times thinking he was falling off the bed. When I told him he wasn't falling, he would not believe me, and every time I tried to lie him down, he would start calling out that he was falling. He now had this uncontrollable twitching and shaking, and I was getting worried.

I did not sleep much that night and was really worried for his safety. I knew that if it got worse, I would have to ring the ambulance. This was becoming quite dire, but Robert refused to go back to the hospital.

I then started to ask myself why was Robert putting me through this? Look at what this is doing to me? I would cry in the shower every morning; I could not stop thinking of what I should really do next. Do I do what Robert wants or do I trust my stomach and go against him even if he refuses.

On the Wednesday morning, we saw Robert's doctor at the clinic. I explained what had gone on the night before and over the weekend. But Robert always had a sound mind in the mornings and was able to show the doctor that he was ok. The doctor did the usual blood tests, motor neuron tests and of course Robert passed them all. There was nothing more the doctor could say but that he would let him go back to the apartment, but if he deteriorates then ring the ambulance.

That night and into the following morning the game changed. When I went to bed, Robert was thrashing around the bed, twitching, and talking. I could not get any sleep and decided to sleep on the couch. When I checked in on him at 2:15 a.m. and 5:30 a.m., everything was basically ok.

But when I woke up at 9:30 a.m. I found a different scenario. Robert had knocked over the bed side table and spilt the glass of water beside the bed and on the floor. What else I saw, I just cannot describe as I still want Robert to have his dignity, but the bedroom looked like he had gone 12 rounds with Mohammod Ali and he had lost.

At this point, the decision for me was easy. I was now taking the choices and decisions away from Robert. He was past the point of being able to make rational decisions himself and for his own safety I had to step in.

After speaking to the clinic who contacted Robert's doctor, they organised an ambulance to come to our hotel. While we were waiting for the ambulance, I continued to watch Robert hallucinate and knew he did not know where he was. When I told him that the ambulance was here to take him back to hospital, he asked me if he had a choice in this. I looked at him with tears rolling down my face and said "no". Then he replied, "Well that is what this has come to" and I said, "Yes it has. I am now in control of your health not you".

It had been so hard watching the events of the last 48 hours and the only safe place for Robert to be was hospital. If this was heading in the wrong or right direction for Robert, he had to have better care and was not leaving the hospital until I was satisfied that he was able to. He had had nearly two weeks' reprieve from the system but now he was going to have to put up with it again.

Chapter 13

Losing the Fight

Robert was very unsettled when he got back into the palliative care ward. The hallucinations were constant, and the nurses said that they would call me if anything developed through the night. I took the opportunity on their advice to have an early night but cried all the way back to the apartment. I was totally exhausted, and sleep came easily after an emotional day.

But my sleep was broken by a call at 7:45 a.m. It was the hospital advising me that Robert had had the Medical Emergency Response Team up to him during the night. That his blood pressure had dropped to a critically low level and he had been given a dose of pethidine to increase it again. Thankfully, his heart had responded, and they asked me to come to the hospital as early as possible as they wanted to chat to me. I immediately jumped out of bed, gathered myself and my things and jumped in the car.

When I arrived at 8:45 a.m. and walked into Robert's room, he was sitting up eating breakfast and I was greeted with him saying, "Hi babe, how are you?" I was nearly knocked off my feet. This was not the description that I was given over the phone. But this is what could occur on any given day. At one time, Robert could have the medical team in his room, making decisions of what to administer to keep him alive, and then within an hour he could be sitting up in bed. The one thing I was grateful for this morning was that he was very coherent and there were no hallucinations.

The doctors and nurses had decided that Robert needed to go into the Acute Leukaemia ward. The care and administration of drugs that he required was too much for the palliative care nurses, so back we went to a room outside of the nurse's station so that Robert could have a higher level of care.

Apart from the shakes, Robert had a decent day. It had been a better one for the best part of a week, we had some decent conversations, he hadn't had any hallucinations and I was comfortable leaving the hospital that night thinking he might be heading in the right direction.

After a good night's sleep, I received a call at 8:45 a.m. advising me that Robert had had a bad night. At 3 a.m. he had a shaking event that went on for five minutes. Robert was yelling and thrashing around the bed and it sounded like the event that I had seen when he thought he was falling. He had lost consciousness and when he awoke the doctor on call made the decision to sedate him to calm him down. They said he had slept soundly post that, but they would need to understand what was causing this.

Because Robert had been calm and there was no threat of anything more sinister at this time, the nurses said take your time before heading into the hospital and we will call you if he deteriorates. Some people, on receiving a call like that, may have rushed in straight away. But after receiving calls at all times through the night over the last six years when Robert had been in hospital, I knew them saying what they said meant he was resting, everything was good at the moment, and do what you need to do now as he is ok.

I arrived at the hospital at lunchtime and although Robert was shaking, he seemed ok. He was able to talk me through the event that had happened in the early hours of the morning and did describe the feeling of falling off the bed. The way he described it was like a small child scared that his parents weren't there to save him from falling. There definitely was something wrong in his brain and I feared that maybe it was secondary brain cancer.

Within an hour of me being at the hospital the delirium kicked back in. Robert was not hallucinating, it was definitely delirium, as he would tip his head back, start mumbling words that I could not understand and then when I called his name, he would stop and look at me and say what? While I was there the weekend doctor told me that they were going to engage a neurologist. They had also made the decision not to administer any blood products and would just keep Robert's fluids up until they could understand what was happening with Robert's brain.

By the time I left the hospital that night, Robert had been sitting up talking to me, had eaten most of his dinner and I'd helped him do his physio exercises twice. I thought the day had ended up being a decent one and decided to go back to the hotel at around 6:30 p.m. When I was leaving Robert asked me if I was bringing the car around. I said, "No, I was going to get it from the car park." He then proceeded to tell me that was good, as he needed to pack his bags and he would meet me downstairs to go home.

Well maybe the day wasn't ending on a good note! I decided to not correct him, gave him a kiss and a hug and said, "I will meet you downstairs in 10". He said "ok" and I left the hospital crying all the way out, wondering if there was any possibility now that Robert will recover.

The following morning, I was woken at 5:15 a.m. by the nurse on the ward advising me that Robert had had tremors for most of the night and they had called in the Medical Emergency Response Team. The MERT had calmed him a little, but they wanted to know if I wanted to come in. I asked if there was an immediate threat to his life, they said they did not know, so I asked them to monitor his situation and call me if it gets worse.

At 6:00 a.m. I received a second call. Robert had been given a dose of medication to ease the tremors and now he was unresponsive. They told me they just wanted to keep me up to date with the treatment and if I wanted to come in I could, but they were not ringing me to get me in.

When the doctor called me at 8:00 a.m., it was time to jump out of bed and get to the hospital asap. The doctor had been called in and Robert was unresponsive, the shaking and tremors had continued even though he was unconscious and the doctor wanted to increase his medication through an automated dispenser that would ease Robert's tremors and keep him calm. I agreed to the treatment and was in the car driving to the hospital within 15 minutes.

I knew this was not good as Robert had not been sedated since April when we thought he was going to die. On the way to the hospital I rang Kyran as I needed someone with me if the doctor had bad news. I also rang my mum and dad. They were up at our house, two hours away, but mum told me they would be on their way as soon as possible.

Losing the Fight

When I arrived at the hospital, Robert was still shaking. The medication had not taken affect yet, but the nurses reassured me that hopefully in the next 15 to 20 minutes Robert would be in a calm state.

Kyran arrived at the hospital within 10 minutes of me and Robert still had the tremors. Both Kyran and I stood on either side of Robert holding his hand saying things like "it will be ok", "the shaking will stop soon", "we are here for you now", and "we love you". We had tears rolling down our faces and it was very distressing to watch.

Thankfully, the tremors did stop within 20 minutes and Kyran and I sat on either side of the bed holding Robert's hand and reassuring him we were both there. I did not know whether he could hear us, but I talked to him as if he could. The doctor came in to see me and gave me the advice that Robert was not going to recover from this, and that we should consider stopping his treatment and move him to full palliative care. I asked the doctor if, before we made that decision, he could speak to Robert's treating doctor. I knew it was the weekend, but I did not want to make that decision unless he was consulted.

Robert's doctor called back. He did not want to stop the reactive treatment and he would assess Robert himself tomorrow. I was happy with this decision as Robert's doctor had treated Robert for the last six years. He had seen Robert nearly die a couple of times and he had seen him rally again. He wanted to give Robert every chance to rally if that is what he is going to do which would allow Robert to make the decision of whether he wanted to live or die.

My parents arrived and during that day Kyran, mum, dad and myself talked through the afternoon. We had lunch together, cried together and laughed together. The one thing any nurse on any ward that Robert had ever been in said was that the atmosphere in his room was usually in good spirits. My friends and family, whenever they visited, always made sure to make it a pleasant experience for Robert, and it also made visiting Robert, especially that day, a little easier on all of us.

Whatever time I arrived at the hospital the following day, Robert's condition had changed a little. Robert seemed to be trying to communicate with me, but I just kept saying to him, "Its ok, you don't need to talk just rest". Robert's doctor came in once the nurses told him that I had arrived, and he started to do some neurological tests on Robert. He looked in his eyes, felt his legs. He first asked Robert if he could squeeze his hand, he did it on the right side after about 3 asks but on the left, he could not do it all. He then asked Robert a couple of questions, but Robert was not responding the way I would have expected.

Robert's doctor told me he would give Robert another 24 hours on the current treatment regime and assess it tomorrow. He could not give me any sureties either way but said things had deteriorated over the weekend and if I needed him to ask the nurses to call him.

The palliative care doctors came and spoke to me as well. They were gentle with their words, but also up front with the situation. They said the next 24 hours would be a critical time and wanted to make sure I had informed the family of the reality and possibilities in case the next phone call was going to be the hardest I would ever make. They were such a wonderful team. I had known them for nearly two months now and they had been by my side this whole time always looking after me.

I rang my parents and informed them of what Robert's doctor and the palliative team had told me. I told them not to come down as John and Di were visiting today and there is not much change from the day before. Mum really wanted to be there but understood.

I then rang Robert's mum and gave her the overview. She didn't ask many questions and I hoped she understood the criticality of her son's condition. I reassured them that I would ring them if anything further happened. Robert's mum always thanked me for keeping them updated, for being by her sons' side and said she would pray that Robert would come out of this and recover again.

But my thoughts were now becoming less confident and although I had not actually conceded that this may be the end of Robert's life, in some way I was trying to prepare myself for the worse.

John and Di arrived and they could see a considerable change in Robert. He was only half the man that they remembered and were quite concerned with what the future held. As I have said previously, these friends are the friends that you will have for life. They loved both of us so much and if they could find a way to take all the worry and pain away I know they would. Just them being there that day, sitting with me was more than I could ask of them.

At different times through the day, Robert was trying to talk, and I kept reassuring him he did not need to talk and just to rest. But when we came back from lunch, he was quite restless. I stood next to him leaning into him, holding his hand, trying to calm him down. He was saying a few words and I could understand him saying "love, I love". I knew he was trying to say I love you and I would repeat it back to him, "I love you too babe, its ok, I love you too." But he kept repeating it over and over again.

Then he was saying something that I thought was "I drive". I looked at Di who was standing on the other side of the bed. "I drive", he said again. Then he took my head in one hand, pulled me down to him and kissed me so passionately. He had never done this the whole time he had been in hospital. Tears started flowing down my face, as they are now as I write this. I smiled through my tears and said, "I love you. I will love you forever, until eternity."

Robert smiled back at me and I sat down on the seat next to him, crying with my hand in his and there seemed to be a love in the room that had never been there before.

I did not realise it at the time or maybe I did not want to hear it, but what Robert was trying to tell me was "I die". He was trying to tell me he was going to die. He was saying goodbye to me. I do not know whether I just did not want to hear that word on that day, or because of the circumstances that then came over the next week. But it took me a few days to recognise what he had said to me. The love of my life had made the decision to die.

Through the last six years, neither Robert nor I had truly acknowledged that Robert's life would come to an end so soon. We always believed in his strength, courage, resilience, and that this disease would never win. But that afternoon with our best friends sitting beside us, Robert confessed his love for me, kissed me like he did on our wedding day and told me that the fight was over. His body had been telling him for days, if not weeks, that it could not endure any more, but now his mind had conceded and he had said the words aloud.

We all sat in silence for some time. I never asked John and Di what they heard. We were all stunned by Robert's actions and we all sat with our minds telling us different things. All I know that even though there was love all around us, there was a deep sadness and pain that none of us wanted to talk about.

On the 4th of June, the following day, I was woken early by my phone ringing, I cannot recall the time, but it must have been around 7 a.m. It was the ward, and they were asking me what time I would be in at the hospital. Robert's doctor had already reviewed Robert's condition and wanted to see me. I told them around 10 a.m., but they asked me to come in sooner. As I was driving to the hospital, I received a second call asking what time I would be in. The palliative care doctors had also been in and they wanted to see me too. The butterflies in my stomach were doing back flips. My mind was going a hundred miles an hour and I did not have a good feeling about this.

I walked into the ward, and Robert's nurse said they would call the palliative care doctors immediately. I went in to see Robert. He was resting soundly and looked at peace. The Palliative care doctors were in the room before I knew it and started to give me the news that I did not ever want to hear.

Overnight, Robert had stopped having fevers. I had heard it said that when a person in Robert's condition stops having fevers it means they have given up, that the immune system cannot fight anymore - Robert could not fight anymore.

I put my hands over my mouth and tears flowed down my face. I couldn't breathe, and I had a pain in my heart that I had never felt before. The only thought I had was that Robert was going to die. His fight was over, he just could not fight anymore. His words yesterday were his words of goodbye and now I had to come to the realisation that this was it.

I was devastated. I looked over at Robert and could not believe that this was happening. The doctors said they will now need, with my agreeance to turn off all the equipment, to move Robert back to the palliative care ward where he would live out his last days.

I remember the calmness in their voices. I also remember saying to them how do I make this decision; how do I make the decision and tell his family that I made this decision. The doctors said, you do not have to make the decision we are making the recommendation and Robert has made the decision.

I understood that this had to happen. I had known other families through the years that had heard these words and made that decision. Some of these families had made the decision with their loved one, who were conscious and able to speak it themselves. But Robert was not able to tell me that morning, although I knew that he did tell me the previous day and now I had to honour his wishes.

I then sought the advice of the doctors on how I was going to tell Robert's parents. Again, they were amazing, giving me the words that would enable me to make the second hardest phone call in my life. They then got me a cup of tea, notified the nurses and said they would call Robert's doctor and tell him they had spoken to me.

Robert's doctor was consulting in the clinic next to the hospital that day, so it was convenient for him to come over and see me. As I was walking to the visitors lounge in the ward, I saw Robert's doctor approaching me. As soon as I saw him, tears flowed from my eyes. He immediately took me in his arms and hugged me. He said, he was so sorry and just continued to hug me tight until I pulled away.

Robert and his doctor had at times acted like mates. I knew that this would be hurting his doctor too. Like any haematologist and oncologist, they know the odds, and a cure is not always possible, and that keeping the patient doctor distance is part of their job. But it seemed different with Robert and him, and I could see the pain in the doctor's face as he told me about the fevers. He told me that Robert's pulse and blood pressure were normal for the first time in months and that his breathing had now eased.

These were all signs that Robert had raised the flag and announced to the medical staff that his time was up, and he was ready to depart this world. He then asked me if I needed anything. I said "no, I'm ok" and I now needed to inform Robert's parents. He told me if they did not understand anything that he was happy to call them himself. I said that should not be necessary and thanked him. He said he would continue to oversee Robert's condition while he was in the hospital. I was incredibly grateful for that and with red eyes and a pain in stomach I went into the visitor's room to start making the calls.

**Robert and I, May 2019 –
Our last photo together**

Chapter 14

Till Death Do Us Part

The first call was to my parents. I do not need to tell you what I said to them, but they were devastated but more they were so sorry that I had to go through this. They could not do anymore for Robert and their total focus was on me. Mum told me that they would be on the road soon and be by my side for whatever time it took.

Now for the hard call. I remember hearing every ring of the phone to Mrs Gomes phone until I heard her say, "Hello, Suzanne". It was the same tone in her voice as always. Always hopeful and positive. But as soon as I heard her voice, my throat closed up, tears welled in my eyes, and it was so hard to speak. Once she heard me say, "Hello, Mrs Gomes". She knew straight away by my tone that all was not good, that this was the call she never wanted to take.

I think she then responded with, "Oh good God, what has happened, how is Robbie?" I then had to break the news that Robert was not going to make it. At the time I could not say the 'D word': "die". I could only say that Robert was going to pass. She broke down straight away, I could then hear Mr Gomes crying in the background. He was screaming.

I do not remember the words between us, I just remember the heart break I was hearing on the other end of the phone. These two people that had brought this baby boy, their son, their first born into the world 47 years ago was now having to hear that he was not going to make it. That their prayers and all the friends and family's prayers had not been enough. That they would never see their boy again.

After a few minutes of them gathering their thoughts and asking what had happened, Mrs Gomes then proceeded to tell me that they would not come to Brisbane to see Robert. That they wanted their last memory of Robert to be the one in April when he had rallied for all of us and had been so bright and wanting to fight.

I totally agreed with their decision. They were nearly 70 and I did not think they could bear the emotion of the situation, especially Robert's dad. I knew how hard it was for me, and I was a strong woman like his mother, but for his father I knew that whatever the next few days would bring would be unbearable.

Mrs Gomes also wanted to make sure I was being supported. I told her that I had spoken to my parents, that they were on their way and together we would support each other. I told her I would be in touch and update her daily. She told me how proud she was of me. That I had been a tower of strength for her Robbie and that she could not have asked for a more loving and kinder woman for her son. These words made my heart break, and I was lost for words.

The grief they were going to feel was on a different level to me. I was in so much pain for them and I was very worried about how the next few days, weeks and months would affect them. We said our goodbyes, conveyed our love for each other and hung up. I immediately dialled Robert's sister told her the update and while we cried together, I then asked her if she could go and see her parents as I was worried about them.

The calls then continued one after another. I rang my sister-in-law, Kim, Robert's brother's wife, to inform her. Jason, Robert's brother, was about to go overseas for work, and I knew he would contemplate whether this was the right thing to do or not. When I spoke to him, I told him to do what is right for you. Robert would not want you to alter your plans for him. You cannot do anything here, you do not need to be up here, but in the end its your decision. I cannot make that for you.

In the end, Robert's brother did go overseas. It was a major work trip for him, across many countries, and I did not know how long Robert was going to live for. I had heard of people lasting a few days, some people a week, but that was up to Robert and who knew with my husband. At times he was a man of mystery and all I could promise is that between Kim and I, we would keep him updated and he would be across his brothers' condition.

I then rang my brother, my best friend, Meagan, Di, Kyran, Heinke, Colleen and my cousin, Rachel. They were the beautiful people that had supported us and who would give me the strength to get through this horrendous time. All the calls were heart breaking. My eyes were stinging, my stomach was turning in circles. It took well over an hour to make all the calls.

I then sent a message to several friends that read:

Hi, family and friends

I am sorry to let you know that Robert has deteriorated overnight and with the doctor's guidance Robert's treatment has stopped.

He is now in the palliative care ward where they have made him comfortable and he is pain free.

I know this is a sad time for not only me but of you. You are our closest friends, and we could not have gotten this far without your messages, support and love.

My heart is breaking but I will not let Robert suffer anymore.

The outpouring of love and pain from near and afar as this message continued to be read throughout the day was heartbreaking. In some cases, it was in disbelief, there was a lot of pain and sadness, but there was also lots of love and support for me. Messages of how much they loved me, how proud they were of me, how strong I was, how lucky Robert was to have me by his side and how much he loved me. There were also lots of prayers and virtual hugs. They all meant a lot to me at this time and every message pained my heart.

All through Robert's six years of treatment, I had always kept everyone up to date. Sometimes the messages were strong, and I made out everything was good when it was not. But over the last couple of months I was more honest with the people who loved us, who loved Robert. I could not sugar-coat it anymore. They needed to know the truth which then prepared them for the message that I sent them that day.

Robert was transferred to the palliative care ward after all his lines were removed and they made him comfortable. It was a corner suite, if that is what you could call it. It had a sofa bed/couch in there that would accommodate me and two big bright windows which would bring the sun in and shine on Robert every morning.

My parents arrived that afternoon and so did Heinke and Robert's favourite nurse. It was so wonderful to have these beautiful humans with me. They filled the room with love, and I felt supported by all of them.

My parents stayed in the Leukaemia Village which is where Robert and I would have been staying if he was having outpatient care. The village is an amazing space for families to stay when their loved ones are in hospital or having treatment. All the families live outside of Brisbane and the village is provided free of charge to them. I was lucky that I could have my family close by staying here and have no concerns for them.

For the next week, Robert's room would be my home away from home. I would sleep in the not so comfortable fold out bed. I would've put up with lying on the floor if it meant spending the final days and hours with my husband. I did not know what it was going to be like. I did not know what to expect. I just knew that I would go with the flow over whatever time I had with my husband. I would make sure he was comfortable and that he knew how much I loved him and will continue to love him.

When I got to be alone with Robert, I always started our conversation with how much I loved him. That he had been so strong for so long and he did not have to be strong anymore. That he did not have to hold on for too long and I was supporting his choice to spread his wings and leave this world. Robert had a tattoo on his upper back, and to me it resembled wings. When I told him to spread his wings, I would refer to that tattoo. That he had chosen to have his wings drawn on him many years ago in preparation for this time.

I also talked to him about all the great memories we had. When we first met, our wedding day. The amazing countries we travelled too. The many gifts he had given to me, the beautiful jewellery, the houses we had lived in and the cars we had driven. I was thankful for the biggest gift that he had given me, our beautiful property in Coolabine. That myself and our dogs would live out a life that was full of happiness. That all the hopes and dreams we had for our property I would fulfil, including building the cabin business. That I would learn how to make it all work, I would be the perfect host and he would be so proud of me.

I also spoke to Robert about what I was going to miss. That I would miss our conversations. I would miss watching television with him, especially him yelling at the footy even when it was not the Kangaroos playing. I would miss our debates and him calling out "Suzanne" in a tone that only our closest friends and family would know.

That I would miss gardening with him and him teaching me how to use a chainsaw and all those tools in the shed. That I would miss our dinners for two, sharing a bottle of red wine on a Sunday afternoon and our Sunday night curries. I would miss not having another photo with Robert, although I was fairly sure he would not miss the selfies, and I would miss visiting our family, seeing him play with our nieces nephews and god children and making everyone laugh.

But, most of all, I would miss not waking up next to him in bed. Sharing our beautiful view where our dreams would be made. Our goodnight and good morning kisses and the warmth from his hugs. It was now that I realised, I would never make love to my husband again and that broke my heart.

There was going to be so much I would treasure that we would not do again, and I could not thank Robert enough for choosing me, giving me 22 years of his life, his soul, his guidance and his love. There will never be another love as strong as ours, there will never be another Robert in my life, he will always be in my heart and our love will never die.

During the night, I would hear the nurse and an orderly come in to turn Robert. It would occur every four hours and they would be so quiet, trying not to disturb me. But I did not mind, they were so gentle with Robert, they would talk to him when they were turning him, telling him what they were doing and comforting him too. There were some amazing people in this world, and I have been lucky to meet so many in the medical industry.

On the second afternoon that Robert was in palliative care, I rang my in-laws and put them on speaker so that they could talk to Robert. They told him how much they loved him. How proud they were of him and talked about several stories from when he was a child. Robert was an only child for eight years until his brother was born, so he had been spoilt by his parents during that time. The stories made me smile and warmed my heart.

Sometimes in life not everything is resolved, and this was a time that Robert's parents wanted to gain his forgiveness for things that had happened between them in the past. They were begging for their son's forgiveness before he departed. My heart was breaking for them. They had carried all this emotion around with them for 25 to 30 years. They were crying and saying sorry repeatedly. It was the most painful conversation I have ever heard.

While they were on the phone, I told them that Robert could hear them, and I knew Robert had forgiven them. I also told them that this happened many years ago and their relationship had gotten so much closer since Robert had been diagnosed with leukaemia. I knew

Robert was listening because Robert's breathing would change on certain conversations. Throughout that week I saw it occur at least once a day, and it was happening right now.

They also said they would miss Robert's phone calls. Since Robert had relapsed, he had started to ring his parents after every appointment. They would talk about the outcome, what his treatment was going to be and then chat about family, the grandchildren and what we were doing. It was so nice to see that they were able to have such a loving relationship from afar. I was so happy that I had made the call to them, and they were so happy that they had the opportunity to talk to their son one last time.

Two days after Robert went into palliative care, a few interstate guests arrived to visit him. My brother, Paul, Robert's best mate, James, and Meagan's husband, Shane, flew up from Melbourne. Their trip to Brisbane had been planned a couple of months before. Their intention was to come up and under Robert's supervision, build a new fence around the front lawn so the dogs were secure, install a couple of gates and build a retaining wall.

It still blew me away that the timing of all this now coincided with Robert being in palliative care and being with his best mates. As now they were able to say their goodbyes in person.

My dad picked them up from the airport and I told him to prepare them for what they were going to see. All of them had not seen Robert for at least nine months. He was a picture of his former self and he was unconscious. But it would not matter how my dad, or I described Robert. Nothing would prepare them with what they saw when they walked in the room.

I walked up to all three of them. Paul and Shane were already crying, and James had tears welling in his eyes. They were so sad, sad for me and in shock. I held Shane for quite some time. Shane is a very emotional person, and even though this was breaking his heart, he would not want to be anywhere else.

Shane and Robert had become friends because of Meagan's and my friendship. They had been friends for over 20 years. Shane was not only proud that they were mates, but he loved the relationship Robert had with his two daughters, as they loved Robert like their second dad. Just before we moved to Brisbane Robert got Shane to play in his indoor cricket team and from there their friendship became even stronger.

My brother had loved Robert like a blood brother. Robert was his mentor, his confidant, his mate and everything else in between. Paul had been with Robert when he bought my engagement ring. Paul had re introduced Robert to his love of athletics by encouraging him to go back to professional running. He would also encourage Robert to play Australian Rules Football with him in three different teams. A passion that Robert had throughout his childhood that he never played himself. He would show Paul how to build structures and use tools that Paul had never used before. I was so grateful that they had this brotherhood that was beyond our relationship.

James had been Robert's best mate from high school. They went to the footy together, both barracking for the Kangaroos, they drank together, and they had drunk a lot over the years. They had been each other's best mans and Robert had loved James' two sons like they were his own. Robert and James had played mixed netball, indoor cricket together and both had a love of Holden V8s. They were great mates and had been through the good and bad times together.

The guys sat around reminiscing and telling the stories that sent us all into fits of laughter for hours on end. The drunken nights, the fights that Robert had broken up. The stories that convinced someone of something stupid, of Robert's moments with their kids and especially the trips away that we had had with each family.

The laughter was dialled up a notch when Steve arrived. We met Steve when he was married to our friend Ruth. When we moved to Brisbane there was not a week or two that went by that we were not wining and dining together. There was a man crush between Steve and Robert that everyone loved. Robert was Steve's security guard and trusty adviser. Steve had been given many a wise talking to or word over their years of friendship. Even when Steve got married, Robert was given the job from Steve's mum, Ally, to watch Steve the night before and make sure he did not get into any trouble. There had been trips away, laughter and tears. Steve just took the stories and laughter to another level.

Now, in a room the size of a small lounge, we had Robert in the bed, and four adult men laughing until tears rolled down all of our faces. My parents, Heinke, Di and I were there too, and the room was filled with such happiness and joyfulness for a couple of hours. There were so many stories that crossed over into each of our lives. There were so many stories that everyone knew about. There was just so much love and laughter when it came to Robert.

The nurses came in several times to check on Robert while they were there, and they were always greeted with laughter and smiles. They loved coming into the room and witness the celebration of one person's life, which told them Robert was an incredibly special person. As I looked around the room with such love in my heart for these beautiful people, I had to wonder if Robert might have arranged this day!

Then it was time for my dad and the guys to head back to Coolabine. The goodbyes were extremely hard to watch and then I had to tell my dad to say his goodbye as he may not get the chance again. He had wanted to come back down over the coming days, but I told him he should not. That he needed to be with the guys, they would keep his mind occupied and someone had to supervise these three if I were not there.

I took a photo of my dad leaning over Robert's bed. I do not know what dad said to Robert but I know he would have said he loved him, he was so grateful for what he had given and done for our family, for him and his wife, Pat, and that he was so proud of him.

After the guys left the room, it went from the boys in the pub back to calm and serenity. My cheeks were saw, my eyes were stinging, and my heart was glowing. I was so happy that the guys and Robert had had these last few hours together. They would remember this day forever.

The other gesture that was so beautiful was the way Heinke and Di worked out a plan to enable my mum to be supported in Brisbane when my dad returned to the property. They worked out that both would come to Brisbane for two nights, stay with my mum. Take her to and from the hospital and keep her company.

It was also great for me; it meant the three of us would be together at one point or another. They would bring me coffee or breakfast in the morning, and we had lunch and dinner together in the hospital restaurant. Mum was always worried that I would not be eating properly, so it was a way mum could be with me, support me and my two beautiful friends would be supporting her.

The one thing I cannot emphasise enough is having a genuine support system in place with family and friends. At a time like this and over the last six years, I have mostly ensured I had the people that I wanted with me when times get tough. You can never expect that you can do it all yourself which I learnt over these years.

It was not just Robert who needed the support during this week. I needed it, and I knew my parents did too, not to mention Robert's parents, so I always made sure there were family and friends in Melbourne supporting them. Your nearest and dearest will always be there for you, working together to make sure you don't have to worry about anything. I can't thank Di, Kyran and Heinke enough for what they did for me over these two months. I will forever be grateful to them.

The other visitor that hopped on a plane when they found out Robert was dying was his mate, Darren, known as Baz. I was surprised when Baz messaged me saying that he was flying to Brisbane that day. Like Robert's other mates, Baz could not believe what he was seeing, and I could see he was visibly shaken when he saw Robert. Baz and Robert had been friends since primary school. They had played soccer together and went to the same high school with James. Baz had read a poem at our wedding and we had also been there for Baz at his wedding.

When Sunday came around, we could not believe that Robert was still holding on. By now he had not eaten anything for over a week or had any fluids since Tuesday morning. His breathing had changed and gotten shallower and every time I asked the nurses, "Is this it? Will Robert pass soon?" They would say, "No, he is just making himself heard. You will know when it happens."

I had never seen anyone die. I had only ever seen one dead person who I accidentally glimpsed lying in the room next to Robert's on Mother's Day that year. I knew what colour he would turn and how he might look. Other than that, the only person that I had ever seen in a state close to death was my grandpa.

That afternoon we were talking to one of the nurses and she was asking what Robert would be holding on for. I was a little dumb founded.

Everyone who was visiting had visited. No one else had said they were coming up. Then I realised that Robert had not had a shave in over a week, maybe two. Robert was always clean-shaven for any event, especially when it came to putting a suit on. He knew me well enough that I was going to dress him in a suit when he was buried, so having a shave was necessary.

I got a razor, a tray of warm water, wrapped a few towels round Robert's neck and started to shave him. I started off a little nervous. I had only shaved Robert a couple of times and when I had he was conscious or able to tell me what to do. Plus, I did not want to hurt him.

I managed to get it done without cutting him and when I was fussing about trying to get all the hair out of his ear, blowing in his ear continuously, Robert's breathing began to change. It started to get heavy and faster and I began to realise he was getting frustrated with me.

Once I realised this, and so did my mum and Heinke, I started to apologise and tell him I was done. That I would leave him alone and go and clean up. Within five seconds of saying this Robert's breathing started to ease. If I were not there, I would not have believed it. I now believed that Robert would have heard everything that was said in the last six days while he was lying in the bed unconscious. The nurses and doctors say people do. Well, now I believe it too.

That evening I told mum and Heinke to leave earlier than the previous nights. It was around 7:30 p.m., they were exhausted, so was I and I just wanted to spend some time with Robert alone.

Over the next couple of hours, we watched our favourite TV shows, and I felt a real sense of calm and peace that I hadn't felt when everyone was with us. I talked about the shows to Robert as I knew he could hear me. I held his hand whilst I told him how much I loved him, how I would honour my promises. I reminisced about the wonderful holidays we had had and the amazing time we had in the Maldives.

I also took the opportunity to take a couple of pictures, of my hand on top of his. We had this photo taken the day we were married with our wedding certificate underneath. It was a time that I remember making all those promises to have and to hold, in sickness and in health from this day forward. So, I wanted to have that same photo before Robert died.

Robert and I were an affectionate couple. We always held hands when we were out. Whether it was at the shops or strolling along the river in Brisbane or going out to dinner. I loved holding Robert's hand, it made me feel safe, loved, and proud to have this man in my life. And now sitting in the hospital room and for many hours over the last 6 years in hospital rooms I had always held his hand.

As the hours passed by, it was time for bed. Although I did not know it then, this would be my last night sleeping in the same room as my husband. On this night, I didn't feel any different to the previous nights and, after getting myself ready for bed, I kissed Robert goodnight.

I tossed and turned through the night because the bed wasn't that comfortable. I could hear Robert breathing every time I woke which was also soothing and rocked me back to sleep.

At 5:30 a.m. I awoke quite sharply and turned to hear Robert take one almighty breath. I jumped out of bed, held his hand, and waited. I waited for about 45 seconds as I did not hear another breath. I pushed the buzzer and the nurse came in. I told her I thought Robert had gone. She checked his pulse and then a second breath was heard. This would be his last. Again, the nurse checked his pulse and, with a whisper, she said he had passed.

I stood there waiting for the next breath, but it never came. I was hoping this was not the end, but it was. Robert had woken me from my sleep to say his last goodbye.

I had always been quite scared of watching Robert die, but now I am so grateful that I had witnessed his passing, that he had given that to me. My amazing, loving, sexy, smart husband of 19 years was gone. He had been so brave for so long, and his time on earth had come to an end.

The nurse said I could have as much time as I wanted to say my goodbyes. I sat next to Robert touching his arm and crying. Sobbing whilst telling him how much I loved him. Looking at him while the colour drained from his face and his skin became cold.

I opened the blinds in the room for the last time so that the early morning sun could shine on Robert's bed. It was like the light was coming from heaven and showing him the road to get there. I did not think I would need much time with Robert but now it seemed that I did not want to leave him.

After a few minutes of watching Robert, I knew it was time to make the calls. I would ring my mum first so that her and Heinke could pack up the unit and meet me at the hospital.

The second call was to Robert's parents. I am sure when the phone rang at 5:40 a.m. that they knew it would be me on the other end. I told Robert's mum that Robert had died peacefully in his sleep and the screams and sobbing on the other end of the phone were heart breaking. They had just lost their oldest child, their first-born, and I knew the pain would be excruciating for them. There was nothing I could say or do that would help them right now. I just felt so sad for them at a level I never thought I could feel.

From Wife to Widow

Then it was call after call. Robert's brother's wife, Kim, as Jason was overseas. Robert's sister, Fiona, was in Japan so I sent her a message. My brother, my best friends and the list went on. Every call as hard as the first. Every call hearing the sobs on the other end of the phone. Everyone sending their love and condolences. I knew every person would be crying their eyes out when I hung up the phone and I hoped that they would all be comforted by their own families as their amazing friend was gone and life would not be the same for them either.

Mum and Heinke arrived with big hugs and tears. They both went to Robert's side, whispered sweet words as tears rolled down their faces. We were all so sad, so heart broken, in so much pain. The nurses were amazing they just let us have our time. They put a picture of a lily on the door which indicated that a person had died.

By 8 a.m., I was ready to leave. I had to make the two-hour drive home with mum and I knew I could not stay in the room forever. While I was showering, Robert's doctor had dropped by and went to Robert's beside. I am sure he would have said something to Robert and possibly said he will miss him. They had such an amazing relationship and Robert's doctor would be hurting that day too.

It was then time to go home and Heinke and mum said their goodbyes and left me alone with Robert to say mine. I do not remember what I said, I am sure there were many remarks of "I love you" and "I will miss you". By now, Robert's body was cold and his eyes were still open. The nurses had said they would close within a few hours of Robert dying but of course, typical Robert they had not, he always hated being predictable.

As I tried to close them, they would not budge. I gave a small laugh between the tears and said to Robert, "of course, you are still doing this your way and you must want to see the road you are travelling on."

As I walked away from the bed, I could not believe the pain and sadness I was feeling. I had never felt like this ever. Even writing this the words cannot describe how I was feeling. All I know is that when I shut the door behind me for the very last time, I threw myself into my mum's arms and sobbed. I cried like I have never cried before, and maybe ever again. The realisation that I never ever get to see my husband again had hit me and the pain was so unbearable.

As the tears flowed, my mum and Heinke hugged me. We stood in the hallway for a couple of minutes while I let the emotion pour out of me. I could not think of anything at this moment in time, I cannot think of anything now. It was just pure pain that I would not wish on anyone.

It was then time to thank the nurses and doctors on the ward. There were warm hugs and they were so thankful that they could care for such an amazing man, and care for me over the last week. These medical staff are the kindest people on this earth and have the most loving caring nature of any nurses I have met.

It was then time to take the elevator, walk the halls of the hospital and find the car for the last time. I do not remember much of the drive home on the 10th of June 2019. Most of the two-hour trip home was spent in silence. I did receive a couple of phone calls from some family although most people that weren't in the inner sanctum weren't aware that Robert had died that morning.

Arriving home was going to be hard. I had my dad, brother, James and Shane at our house. They had been there for the last four days building fences and retaining walls, completing Robert's wishes. They were some of the closest friends Robert had and now I had to face them, their grief, my grief. I pulled up and their faces were long, sad and exhausted. These four men were heartbroken that their mate had lost the fight. They all gave me their condolences, the biggest hugs and we all cried together.

For the remainder of the day I was numb. Probably actually in shock. I don't remember any of the conversations. I don't remember doing a hell of a lot during the day. I remember checking in on my in-laws. I knew they weren't going to be great; they were so distraught when I rang them earlier that morning, but I wanted them to know they weren't alone and I was continuously thinking of them.

I made the 10th of June a tribute day to Robert, and Heinke and Richard joined us as well. We ate Robert's favourite meal, had a few wines, and shared memories and laughs about Robert while sitting around the bamboo bonfire. Robert hated that mound of bamboo and it was one of the first things he cut down when we moved to Coolabine. Now, it was our tribute to him by burning it to the ground.

This plaque hangs in the courtyard of the palliative care ward.

Chapter 15

A Fitting Tribute

The next nine days were consumed with organising Robert's funeral. I had a burial to plan, a reception, photo board, picking out Robert's clothes to wear, and writing a eulogy. I had made the decision to have Robert's body returned to Melbourne and he would be buried at the Altona Memorial Park.

Writing the eulogy, choosing the pictures for the collage, the songs, were relatively easy tasks. When I was working on all of this, it felt like I went into work mode and was delivering the actions as part of a project.

The hardest decision was picking what he would be dressed in. Robert loved to wear a suit. He had so many at home. At least once or twice a year he would buy a new suit for a special event. He had bought a suit last year that he had only worn once so I decided that was the one. He always loved wearing a white shirt so I choose that and seeing the suit was navy I would pair it up with his favourite brown leather boots and belt.

When it came to selecting the tie and pocket chief, well that was a task. Robert again always had a particular way of pairing the two. I kept swapping the tie and pocket chief, one after another and just couldn't get the combination right. By this time, I was talking to Robert, "Talk to me Robert, give me a sign I know there is one combination and I just can't find it."

Then, after I selected the tie and I turned back to his side of the wardrobe, on the floor was the pocket chief that I was looking for. Where had that been, how did that end up on the floor? I said out loud, "Well thank you Robert, this is the combination." My man was going out in style.

I also included the superman pin that his god-daughter, Caitlin, had sent up to him when he was in palliative care. Everyone called him their superhero, but for Caitlin, the significance of him being her Superman was more significant than anyone else.

Six days after Robert had died, my parents and myself boarded the plane to Melbourne, the most painful trip that I would ever take south. I know one day that I will have to take that trip to send off my parents, but this one, sending off my husband at 47 years old made me feel so empty.

My brother picked us up from the airport and because he had been at our house when Robert had died there were no tears. But the sadness on all of our faces of what this week was going to mean was evident. We were all tired, sad and withdrawn and outside of big hugs we spoke about everything but Robert in the car.

From here we went to Meagan and Shane's house as I was staying with them while I was in Melbourne. I selected their house because it was close to Robert's family, the funeral company, and the Memorial Park. Plus, I also knew my best friend would look after me with such love and I needed to give my parents a break.

As we turned into her street, I started to feel ill. I started to shake and it was hard to swallow. As I stepped out of the car in front of their house my palms started to sweat and my eyes filled with tears. Meagan and I had been best friends for the last 43 years. We had been through so many good times and bad times together. I still remember the night when I was 14 that her brother died of brain cancer, the pain she felt at 13 was the pain I knew she would feel again. She got me like no other and she felt my pain like no other too.

As we stepped up to the door, her husband, Shane, was there with my goddaughter, Abby. Both took me in their arms and the tears started to flow. But when I saw Meagan the flow of tears was like a waterfall. She took me in her arms and hugged me so tight; we both cried like we had never cried in each other's arms before. Her embrace told me that she was the perfect person to care of me over the next week and I was so grateful she was with me.

My next embrace was Caitlin, our other goddaughter and, like I said, the one girl that I think loved Robert nearly as much as I did. Robert was her role model, her hero, her number one. He was the first person she loved outside of her mum and dad and the two of them had such a beautiful connection.

My sister-in-law, Katrina, and niece were also at Meagan's house. They both embraced me and gave me their condolences and more tears flowed.

The following day I visited Robert's parents. When Robert's dad opened the door, he was visibly upset and as I hugged both him and Robert's mum our tears began to fall. I could not imagine the pain that they were suffering. Their oldest child, son, had died and nothing could take away their pain. Robert's brother was also back from his trip and was at their house too. His sadness was so evident, he loved and admired his brother. Jason was a strong man, but his face showed pain that I had never seen before.

We also met with the celebrant that day. I knew her from previous family funerals, and she was a reliable, caring and very well-spoken woman. I was so grateful that someone I knew could perform the service and I was confident she would send him off with a beautiful ceremony.

The service would be held in a reception centre because I expected around 200 people would possibly attend. She asked us several questions that would form a chronological reflection of Robert's life. I could see that it was hard for Robert's parents to remember some events, reflections of Robert's life, but they did so well.

I did not ask Robert's parents to organise any of the funeral arrangements. I wanted to make sure that they were happy with what I was planning and that they just needed to care for each other. This was just the start of their grief and I worried that this may take a horrible toll on them.

Over the next two days my time was spent finalising the funeral. Taking Robert's suit to the Funeral Director, buying candles and having a photo enlarged and framed. Creating a memorial card, having Abby complete the slide show and buying a black dress.

When I left home, I did not have an appropriate black dress in my cupboard and needed to purchase one. My goddaughters, Abby and

Caitlin, came with me to buy one and it took us quite some time before we found the right shop to buy the dress. I took five black dresses into the dressing room and found the one that was appropriate for the funeral. It was going to be cold on the day and I needed to be warm too.

When we took the dress to the counter, and after the shop attendant had already seen me with five very plain black dresses, with a happy tone in her voice she said, "What is the occasion?" I looked at the girls and said, "My husband's funeral". I think the woman wished the floor would open and she could slip away. I could not believe she had asked me that and had not taken more notice. I was glad I made her feel uncomfortable and hope she never puts someone in that position again.

The last task to organise was to meet the deacon who would perform the catholic blessing at the burial site. The burial would be a private ceremony for Robert's and my immediate family. I did not want 200 people at the grave site, and I knew Robert's parents would be extremely upset at the burial. The deacon was a lovely man, who was also Anglo-Indian, like Robert's family, and Robert's parents felt at ease around him. Although I am not religious and Robert never practised it, I was happy that I had arranged this for them.

The four days in Melbourne so far had been busy. I was happy with everything I had arranged and at the end of the day, I wanted this to be a memorial of reflection, not only of a life lost too soon, but one that bought so much happiness to so many people's lives.

The day of the funeral I was up early. My god daughter and I needed to be at the reception centre by 9am so that I could be at the Memorial Park for Robert's burial by 10 a.m. I felt like the day was flying already and I felt nauseas. I never thought this day would come and I never wanted to bury my husband this early in life. But I was focused on the task, that was until I got to the burial site.

Robert's family and mine were already there. We all walked slowly up to his open grave and awaited the hearse to bring the casket. My father in law, my dad, Robert's brother Jason and my brother Paul all walked over to the hearse and assisted with carrying the casket to the grave site. I kept looking at the casket, knowing that Robert was in there, but also wondered what he looked like. Had they put him in his suit. Was he laying peacefully, and did he know how much I loved him?

The blessing went well, and my niece Jennifer read out a beautiful message about their Uncle Robert on behalf of her siblings. But when it was time to lower Robert's casket into the grave Robert's mum was extremely distressed. She did not want to let him physically go; she could not bear the sight of her son being lowed into the ground. It was heart breaking to watch and I really felt for her. Robert's sister and his dad helped his mum through the moments that followed. Then, we all dropped a rainbow flower on top of his casket and said our goodbyes.

My heart was in pain. I had never been so sad. It was all overwhelming and I had not even faced the waiting family and friends for the memorial. I now needed to pull myself together as I had a eulogy to conduct.

Walking into the foyer of the reception centre my chest was tight and I was shaking. I went to the bathroom to freshen up and my Auntie Marie and cousin, Rachel, came in to hug me. It was all I needed at this point to walk into the reception room. A little comfort from two amazing family members made a difference.

As I walked into the reception room behind Robert's parents, everyone was staring at me. Giving me small smiles, some coming up to hug me and give me their condolences. It was something I did not think about. How people were going to react to me and how many people were in the room.

People were standing which told me there was somewhere in the vicinity of 250 people here. 250 people that respected and loved my husband and I enough to pay their respects and say goodbye. Wow, it blew me away. Another moment of overwhelming feelings that I did not expect.

The service got under way with one of Robert's favourite songs. It was by The Killers, Robert's favourite band, about a fight between two famous boxers. What a fitting song, a true reflection of the fight that he had been through over the last six years.

The celebrant was wonderful and was so caring and showed real compassion presenting Robert's life. We then had a candle service where a selection of family members, including Meagan Shane and our god daughters went up to the main candle and lit smaller candles and put them in a bowl of sand. This tribute meant that Robert will be lit in our hearts and minds for the rest of our lives.

The collage that our goddaughter, Abby, had put together to our wedding song *From This Moment* was so wonderful. It captured happy photos of Robert doing the things he loved. His smile in the photos were contagious, and it bought smiles to people's faces in the room.

Then it was time for me to read my eulogy. As I stood up and walked to the stage, I had a sick feeling in my stomach and my hands were shaking. I knew my voice would quiver at the start, but this was something I had always wanted to do, whether it be now or when Robert was 80. Today was the day and I was as ready as ever to read out the amazing attributes and memories of my late husband.

Standing up the front I could see so many people that had flown in from Brisbane, had travelled many miles and so many work mates of ours that we had worked with over the years. There were moments in the eulogy that brought laughter and a few that brought tears, but most of all I was so proud that Robert had loved me, selected me to be his one and only for 22 years. That we had shared so many precious moments together.

As I said to all the well wishes who attended, I didn't know that the kiss a week before Robert died would be my last, him telling me that he loved me would be the last time and that I would never feel his touch again. My heart was breaking, but I had fulfilled a promise to myself of conducting the eulogy and I was so proud of doing it.

After a eulogy from my brother and Robert's brother it was time to end the service. The last song I had picked was *Rainbow Connection* by Kermit the Frog. This song was known by so many in the room. When iPods were in vogue, Robert was the music man. He would upload songs onto his family and friends' devices and would include *Rainbow Connection*. When they played their iPod and the song came on, they would start laughing and said "good on you Robert" and "only Robert would do that".

At the time of the funeral I did not realise the impact that song would have on so many people. Now when they hear the song or see a rainbow they think of Robert. *Rainbow Connection* makes the people who knew Robert smile and warms their hearts. Just the way Robert did when he walked in a room.

The most overwhelming part of the day was the fact that everyone wanted to give their condolences to me. Everyone in the reception hall wanted to speak to me and the line that was in front of me was so long. I stood in the same place for at least 90 minutes thanking the well wishes for coming. Thankfully, I had a couple of people bring me something to drink, although I did need a stiff one at that stage.

Overall, the turnout was quite incredible and a reflection of the man Robert was. His kind heartiness, humour, love, care, energy, strength, courage, and respect were coming from everyone I talked to. They also had such respect and care for me. I had so many tears coming out of my eyes that my cheeks burnt, and I was so happy to say the last thank you and close the memorial.

I have conducted several workshops, presentations, speeches, and conversations in my working life, and I would say all them went well and hit the mark. But today was the most rewarding day for me. I was so proud of how the memorial had gone and I hoped that Robert would be so proud of how it came together. I know he would have also said it was over the top, but I am sure he would have loved every minute of it!

After a few drinks with my closest family and best friends, it was time to go back to Meagan and Shane's. It had been an exhausting and emotional day and it was time to put the tracksuit pants on and relax on the couch with a bowl of soup.

I went and stayed with my brother and parents for one night after the funeral and went to see Robert's family before heading home. I was now feeling the effects of the last two weeks and was looking forward to having some time at home by myself with my two dogs to clear my mind. What I didn't know is that is not how grieving works!

In 2018 my brother Paul and I undertook a 10km run on the Gold Coast to raise money for the Leukaemia Foundation

Chapter 16

Life Without Robert

I would not be spending too much time alone when I returned home, as my best friend Meagan was arriving in a week from Melbourne to spend ten days with me. The one thing about Meagan is that she has been there for me in the darkest days. She has such a caring side to her and our friendship which has lasted for 43 years was shining through right now.

It was also going to be great to have her up here as on the Friday night I was having a wake in Brisbane for our friends and family that could not make it to Melbourne. Having her by my side for that and making sure that it went well was also going to be a great support. As I said, she is always there when I really, really need her.

Meagan's words to me when we embraced and started driving back to Coolabine, was I do not care what we do, I have no plans. Whatever you want to do whilst I am here, we will do. A lot of people might say they would do that for you, but their actions do not reflect it. Not Meagan, she stood by her words. Whatever I wanted to do she was with me.

The next few days we hung around the house, went into town a couple of times, and had dinner at Heinke and Richards house. We slept until late and just hung around, which was exactly what I needed.

Then Friday came around and it was time to go down to Brisbane for Robert's wake. We had to pick my mum and dad up from the airport and then head into Woolloongabba where we had our accommodation for the night.

The wake was being held at the Pineapple Hotel, Robert's favourite Brisbane establishment. Over the years we had enjoyed many lunches, dinners, football games, cricket matches and of course lots of beverages there. Whenever we had a free Friday, Saturday night, or Sunday afternoon Robert would suggest that we go there. Whenever we went to the Gabba (Brisbane's AFL ground) we would go there first and every time we had friends visit from interstate, we would take them there. It was his favourite watering hole, so it was only fitting to hold his wake there.

Like the memorial service in Melbourne, I displayed his photo and a few pieces of memorabilia. The wake was held in a room off to the side of the back bar. I put platters out for the guests who were made up of a mix of family, work mates, Unplugged friends, nurses from the Cancer Centre and several friends. The room was full, overflowing, and I was so proud to see that another 60 to 70 people had come to pay their respects and remember Robert.

I conducted Robert's eulogy from the memorial service with a few additional words to personalise the Queensland adventures that Robert had been part of. It was again overwhelming. The laughs occurred at the same passages, and the tears rolled as I neared the end. Again, I was so proud that I had been able to stand up before these amazing people and allow them to grieve and celebrate Robert's life.

The next day, my parents, Meagan and I ventured back home and I had a few more days with my gorgeous friend. Before Meagan left, we had the opportunity to go out to lunch. I cannot remember the context, but there were tears and heart felt conversations. I was going to miss her so much, but my parents were back for two months so I knew I would be well looked after.

When the day came to say goodbye to Meagan, we pulled up at the airport terminal and more tears flowed. I did not want to let her go. I did not want her to go home. I wanted to be around her beautiful, calm and loving nature, but she had her beautiful family to go back to, all of whom were also grieving Robert's death, and she had to go home to them.

I had decided to take a couple of days' reprieve down at John and Di's on the Gold Coast, and having my parents up meant they could look after the dogs and chickens and allow me to visit them. The two nights there was the start of something that I had not thought about. I was now in my own eyes the third wheel. I would be the add on to all my friends.

On the first night we stayed at home and had dinner. It felt completely foreign to sit at the table without Robert sitting next to me. There had only been a handful of times where I had visited John and Di and sat at their table without Robert. We were two peas in a pod. If you had me there, then you had Robert. I commented on this and John and Di acknowledged that they felt the same. We all had to learn to adjust to this new reality.

John and Di had known Robert longer than I had. John met Robert when Robert was 18. A young, very skilled indoor cricketer and John invited Robert to play in his team. Over those years, they had played indoor cricket, had several weekends together up on Johns houseboat on the Murray River, and Robert had been at John and Di's wedding.

John and Di had also been the friends that when Robert had a turn for the worst over the last two months of his life, they had been there. They were the ones that had held me tight, had comforted me while I made those heart-breaking phone calls to the family. John was the one who I talked to about taking Robert's body back to Melbourne. To making the heart-wrenching decisions on whether to stop treatment the first time when I thought I was losing Robert in the April.

They were also the friends that witnessed my last kiss from Robert. They had listened to him a week before he died saying "I die", they would be the last people to hear Robert's words "love you". Heart breaking for not only me, but for them too.

Now, three weeks after Robert's death, I was sitting at their dining table, a setting of three, a setting that would now be the norm for whatever time was necessary. Just the three of us, best friends and healing together over the loss of a great friend. We held our glasses up before the meal and clinched them whilst saying "to Robert!" We knew he would be staring down from above with his own glass of red and although he was not at the table, he would be always there in spirit.

Over the next six weeks my parents and I completed several projects around the house and we went on a couple of day trips too. But most of all we just enjoyed being with each other.

To me, my parents are one in a million. They left their life in Melbourne to be by my side to help me at the saddest and hardest days of my life.

They never asked me how I was going, which I was grateful for, as they could see that in my eyes. Of course, there were some good days and there were also some sad days. But when the sad days occurred, they never asked anything they just allowed me to talk if I wanted to and let me be silent if I needed to.

On the fourth Monday after Robert's death, something unexpected occurred. I was woken up by what I thought was a knock at my bedroom door. I woke up listening for a voice. If mum or dad needed me, I knew they would call my name and then open the door. I sat so still in bed waiting for a noise or voice.

After about five minutes I decided to grab my iPad which was sitting on the bed and look at the time. It was 5:34 a.m., and I would have been lying in bed for those four minutes waiting to hear a sound. Whether it was my brain playing tricks on me or the spirit of Robert reminding me he was here, that knock that I heard was at 5:30 a.m. on Monday morning, four weeks after Robert had died. The exact time that Robert had died.

On that morning, or maybe the next morning my dad recalled a moment where he heard a voice. He awoke after hearing what he thought was Robert saying, "Are you awake Noel?" Dad sat up and said, "Who's there?" He then woke up mum and asked her if she had said it, which she had not, she had been sound asleep. Dad said he heard Robert's voice and it had unnerved him at first, but then felt humbled that Robert had visited him too.

There were many mornings over that six-week timeframe that I did not want to get out of bed. The nights were the hardest and I would go to bed, shut the door and lie there crying. I hated bedtime. It was so lonely in that big king size bed. I missed Robert's embrace and the way he would hold me when we initially went to bed.

On one occasion, I had finished crying, turned off the lamp and got into my usual position. I then felt this cool breeze shoot across my face. My two-bedroom doors were closed and although I had my dogs sleeping in the room with me, they always slept on the floor. There was no way a breeze could come through my bedroom. Again, I put it down to Robert laying with me and breathing on me. For me it was a reminder that he was always going to be with me, by my side.

Now I know people are sceptical of the spirit world. They do not believe in it and cannot be convinced of it, and that is alright. But I am open to any possibility and when you are grieving you sometimes just want to believe that your loved one does venture off into some other world. That they can watch you from above, continue to protect you and still give you signs that they are around.

For me, that is what I wanted to believe. I could not believe anything else because then I could not understand why Robert had left me so early in our lives. He continues to watch over me, guide me and continue to give me a sign that he was right there with me. It was a way of me being able to function in some sort of normality at a time where normal was a distant memory.

Over the next year, outside of the stories I tell in this book, grief would hit me unexpectedly. When I heard a song, when I watched a tv show, when I was in the car. I have had moments when I would just cry and cry. Although 16 months on I still have those moments, I feel that the length and frequency of them is getting less.

I have also found that at times, while I am talking about Robert, some people get uncomfortable and don't know how to respond. At first, I saw that as rude and disrespectful. But I am learning not to be offended by those reactions. I might not be able to rationalise the reaction at first, but I am trying not to make assumptions and just let go of my reaction to their reactions.

Grief for a loved one can never be explained or understood until you go through it. Even now I never say to someone who has just lost their loved one that I understand. Because frankly I don't. Loss is different for everyone, we all react to it differently, but I do know one thing, loss leaves an empty hole in your heart. Maybe a hole that will never be healed.

You cope with grief and loss, you never get over it!

I have seen several rainbows since Robert has died, and when they are in the valley in front of the house, I know it's Robert saying hello.

Chapter 17

Bad Luck Comes in Threes

The day after my parents went home, I ventured over to Caloundra to pick up a load of sleeper pavers to lay on the new path that the boys had built. That afternoon I started to lay the pavers and because it was where the new gate was, I let my dogs, Jonty and Harry run around the property while I started laying them. Quite a job for one person, let alone me, but I was determined to do the work that I could around the property and become self-sufficient at some things.

Over the course of the next couple of hours, I would check on the dogs, make sure they had not started to go on some sort of adventure. Jonty was nearly three, a Jack Russell-poodle cross, and had a sense of adventure. Coming from the city, his first two years were in a small back yard and only ventured out when I went running or walking. He loved running around the property, and he would have a smile on his face every time he was in the paddocks.

Harry was eleven months old and was highly influenced by Jonty. We had not taken Harry to puppy school as I had bought him the day after we had moved to Coolabine. He was a good dog and did have some discipline in him. But like Jonty, he loved going out beyond our fence lines, following his brother, and run around the property.

It was coming up to 4 p.m. in the afternoon and I was on the phone to my parents. After being on the phone for 30 minutes I realised I had not seen the dogs for a while. I told my parents I better go as I was worried they might have gone on to next door's property, and I had heard from the neighbours that he had threatened to shoot a wandering dog on his property even if it had a collar on. The other reason I was worried was because I knew he was going to be baiting on his property and that the dogs may have ventured over there attracted to the smell.

Farmers work in with the Council to bait and kill wild dogs, which live in the mountains behind my property. You hear them howling at night, I have seen them run across the paddocks of my neighbour's property and once Jonty has chased a dog off my property. They will kill small animals, especially newborn calves, and attack your dogs, especially if they or you have female dogs in heat.

I started walking up and down my driveway and walked out beyond the chicken shed at the back of the house, calling their names and whistling. I could not see them anywhere and I started to worry. After another hour, I started to check in on the neighbours to see if they had seen them. But to no avail they had not been sighted by anyone.

It was now past 6 p.m. and over two hours since they had disappeared. I decided to ring Richard to understand what effect the bait would have on them if they ate it. At the same time, I explained that there was no sign on the fence at the back of my property so I could not confirm if the bait had been laid or not.

The baiting process is controlled, the Council send you a notice to say when the baiting will occur and then around a week or so before the baiting starts the farmer puts signs up for the four week period that the baiting will be happening. In this case, the baiting dates had started but I hadn't seen the signs that were to be erected on my fence to alert me to it.

The farmer needs to keep a record of what they bait and how much and they should bait and ensure it is at least 500 metres inside their own property to try and prevent domestic dogs from smelling it and eating it. After educating myself on the process, I tried to tell myself that they would not have ventured into my neighbour's paddocks, that they had found something to eat and they were enjoying their feast.

Richard told me that his neighbours or the state forest usually drop in additional letters the day before they start just to make sure you are aware it. I had not received anything from my neighbour so at this stage I thought it may not have happened. Richard also told me that if they do return you will know if they have eaten the bait in around three hours. I should start to see signs of them having eaten poison by then.

Then, like too-excited children that had just finished playing for the day and wanting their dinner, Jonty and Harry returned. They ran through the gate coming from the back of the property, with their tails wagging and their tongues hanging out. I told Richard they were back and if anything started to happen, I would ring him.

I told the dogs I was so happy to see them home, that I had been worrying about them, and that I hoped they had not eaten any bait. They had been away from the house for over three hours and I was still concerned. For the next three hours they were inside, sitting, mostly sleeping in the loungeroom while I watch television.

The first sign that Harry gave me that they had eaten something was around 9:30 p.m. He started to dry reach and vomited up what looked like rabbit hair. There was a sense of relief when I saw that hair as after speaking to Richard it didn't sound like farmers baited dead animals like rabbits, and that the dogs must have caught and eaten a rabbit. I rubbed Harry and said to him, cough it all up, get it out and had a smile on my face. This must have been what they had been doing.

At 11:30 p.m., five hours after returning home, with no additional signs of them being poisoned, I decided to put them outside to go to sleep. They were now sleeping in a secured area at the northern end of the house, just behind my bedroom. Dad had built them a dog kennel and they would snuggle in their together.

While I was reading my book in bed, I heard what sounded like howling. I jumped out of bed and went to the laundry door, turned on the light and saw Harry running around the secured area yelping. My heart sank. Oh no, maybe they had eaten the bait. I tried to grab Harry and calm him down, but he was in so much pain and I did not know what to do. So, I let him inside and Jonty followed.

Harry then ran down the hallway to the front door. He was yelping in so much pain and when I turned on the light, I noticed that he was bleeding. Where was this blood coming from? The poor fellow did not know what was happening to him, I was trying to help him but also cautious that he might bite me. Then he came up the hallway and collapsed on the floor in front of the second bedroom.

It was at this stage I decided to ring the vet. I was now crying and wanting to help Harry, to take him to the vet to fix him. But when I spoke to the vet, who was on 24/7 emergency call, he conveyed the bad news. If Harry had consumed the poison bait 1080, which sounded like he had, the only thing he could do for me was ease his pain. There was no anti-vaccine to reverse the poison and that he would die.

I said that I would bring him in immediately and hung up. As I stroked Harry's hair he had started to shake. He was frothing at the mouth and although he was trying to get up his bowels were losing control and I knew I could not lift him. After everything I had been through with watching Robert die, I was now going to see my dog die in front of me too.

I was crying so hard, calling out, "No, Harry, do not die on me. Mummy loves you, I am not mad with you for eating the bait". I was sitting on the floor next to Harry, Jonty was on the loungeroom floor looking at me wondering what was going on. He was coming up to me, but then would sit back down.

Then, in a couple of minutes since hanging up from the vet, Harry stopped breathing. My puppy, my beautiful, gorgeous border collie was dead. What have I done? Why did I let them run around? I should have known better. But all I could do was cry, cry loud and the tears cascaded down my face. I decided to ring the vet back saying my dog had died and I would not be coming in.

I then rang Richard and told him that Harry had died. I was in shock I was so upset and immediately he asked after Jonty. How is he, has he got any signs? I looked at Jonty and said no, he seems ok. Richard was relieved. Richard and Heinke had known Jonty since he was a pup and he held a special place in their hearts too. Richard said they would be on their way immediately and would see me soon.

I sat on the floor next to Harry and just cried my heart out. I could not believe my dog had just died in my arms. In some way the pain in my heart was just as bad as seeing Robert die. But in some ways, it was worse because this had all happened in a matter of 20 minutes, I was blaming myself and what poor Harry had endured was heartbreaking.

I turned my attention to Jonty who was sitting on the rug in the loungeroom watching Harry die. Then Jonty gave me a face that said he had eaten the bait too. The face also told me that he was so sorry that he had led Harry out there. His face was so sad and then my nightmare started again. From the sadness of losing one dog, I then realised I was going to lose the second dog too.

Jonty started to convulse and vomited up what looked like kidneys or liver. He continued to vomit up large amounts of it, which I was so relieved to see. I said to him through my tears, "Vomit it up mate, good boy, get it out and hopefully you will be ok." But he was not going to be ok because then he started to run around the house yelping in pain. All I could yell out was "noooo!" at the top of my voice. Not again.

I then heard the motor of Richards car arrive. He and Heinke jumped out of the car and came through the front door. They were greeted with blood inside the front entrance and then as they took the two steps up to the hallway, they saw Harry laying lifeless on the tiles.

They asked where Jonty was, and I said he had run outside to the front patio. It was here that we found Jonty at the end of the pool, curled up in ball yelping. I went to bend down and pick him, but Richard told me not to, that he might bite me and just leave him be.

There was nothing we could do, and we had to sit this out. By this time, Jonty had run back inside, Heinke shut the door and we watched Jonty start to convulse. He was in the hallway just outside the laundry door and was at the opposite end of the hallway from where Harry lay.

Bad Luck Comes in Threes

Richard then grabbed me, hugging me so tight, and walked me to the lounge. I couldn't speak, I was so overcome with emotion, I was crying my eyes out and rocking backwards and forwards. "No", I kept saying, "No". Richard held me tight as we listened to the excruciating pain that Jonty was going through. For a little dog he was a fighter just like Robert. No wonder he and Robert had such a strong connection. All through Robert's relapse Jonty would sit on Robert's legs or beside him while Robert was in pain. His dad was a fighter and now Jonty was trying to fight his own pain, a battle he was not going to win.

It seemed like what Jonty was going through took so much longer than Harry. Then with one last yelp there was silence. It was all over. In the space of half an hour, 36 hours from when my parents had left here, giving the dogs big pats, saying we will see you soon, both dogs had died. They had eaten poison and I had experienced a loss I was not prepared for.

Heinke sat on the couch and Richard continued to comfort me. All three of us were so upset. Heinke and Richard loved Jonty. He had given them as much joy as us. Jonty had been one of the only dogs that had been allowed to sleep inside with us, at their house. He had warmed their hearts and he loved playing with Chico and Lily, their dogs, and had come with us on many hikes through the Imbil state forest.

But now they were gone, now I was truly alone. My eyes were sore, and my heart was in so much pain. I could not think, I could not get up from the couch. I was numb and sad. Heinke decided to get two towels and put them over each dog. They then made the decision that I would go to their house for the next few nights and Richard, with help of my neighbour would bury the dogs tomorrow.

I packed a bag and we locked up the house. I left my two dogs under pale blue towels at either end of the hallway to grow their wings and meet up with Robert. As we drove the 30 minutes back to Heinke and Richards house, I messaged my neighbour to tell her what had happened and continued to cry. I was in a level of shock and just could not understand why this had occurred. I was still grieving heavily for my husband, and now had to grieve for my two puppies as well.

That night, Richard, Heinke and I sat up until dawn. We sipped single malt whisky chatting. The conversation is not one I can remember, all I know is the whisky helped dry my eyes, and so too did the care and love that I received from my wonderful friends. As we watched the sunrise, eating homemade toast with honey and fresh loose-leaf tea, we smiled at how the simple things in life are often the best. I had been comforted again by two amazing friends, two people that had gone through their own blood cancer trauma, the grief of losing their friend Robert and now losing their surrogate dogs.

After we realised it was 6:30 a.m., Richard rang my neighbour and planned to meet him in half an hour to bury the dogs in the front yard. I was going to make a memorial that represented Robert now that memorial would be a place of burial for my puppies too.

Two months ago, I had bought three roses from a garden show in Nambour, without really knowing why I bought three. The roses were called 'Remember Me' and were a commemorative flower for those that had lost a love one. It was now fitting that I had three to plant on top of where the dogs lay, next to the seat that I talked to Robert from.

Once Richard left, Heinke and I went to sleep. I also uploaded a message on Facebook telling everyone that the dogs had died. I had rung my parents and my best friend Meagan. Everyone was in shock and could not believe that I had to suffer further loss. This world can sometimes be so cruel.

I then was able to cry myself to sleep, and I slept for a couple of hours. During this time, Richard and my neighbour had hand dug a hole, wrapped the dogs up in the towels and buried them. Jonty in between the legs of Harry, cuddled together where they would stay forever. Richard then cleaned up my house and I could not thank him and John enough for taking care of this and not having me to go through further pain.

Later that afternoon, Heinke and I went back to the house so I could pick up some more essentials. I had not packed well the night before which was understandable, and I was going to stay at their place for a second night. During our visit we walked up to the back of the paddock and noticed that there was a sign on the fence. I did not remember that sign being on the fence the afternoon before when I was looking for the dogs. I had walked right up to that area and I am sure I would have noticed it. Because if it was there, I would've ventured into my neighbour's property looking for them.

But it didn't matter now. I could not reverse the events of the previous night and had to live with the guilt that I had let my dogs out even when I knew there was a possible threat.

It took me many months to get over the guilt that I had caused the death of my dogs. I was the one who was negligent, I had to suffer the heart ache. I also came to the conclusion that maybe Robert needed those dogs more than I did. That having to live entirely by myself, without anyone or anything except for my five chickens, that this was wiping the slate clean for a new beginning.

I did tell everyone I was not ready for a new puppy as the pain of the loss was too deep. But fast forward three months and while sitting in Melbourne in Meagan's loungeroom looking for a second dog for them, I started to look up Border Collies in the Queensland/Northern NSW area.

After looking for a while I found two puppies in Northern NSW. They were border collie-Kelpie cross, black and white like Harry, born on the 13th of September. Me with my spirituality saw this as a sign. Robert went into hospital on the 13th of September and was diagnosed with leukaemia six years ago. Maybe this was the dog for me.

I sat on it for a couple of days as I was going to Bali with a couple of friends and I needed to decide before I left. I thought if one were still available, I could possibly pick it up when I returned to Brisbane after Bali. It was only a two-hour drive from the airport, so I made the decision to message the seller. She told me they had one male left and in a matter of seconds I said I will take him. Meagan and the family were so happy, I rang Heinke and told her I have bought a dog and I could not wait to meet him in a week's time.

On the 3rd of December after I flew back to Brisbane, I drove for two hours south into NSW and picked up Archie. He was so adorable, the last of the litter. He was twelve weeks old and was perfect for me. I was in special need of lots of love hugs as living by myself had been difficult. So a new puppy, a new best mate was what I needed.

After a four-hour drive, Archie saw his new home for the first time and over the months to come would evolve into the most loyal, lovable dog that I would ever own. I have told Archie all about his dad and his brothers in heaven and we often sit on the chair next to the boys' memorial and I talk to them.

I don't know what it is with Archie, but he has a sense of knowing when a person is in pain and gives them so much attention. I believe Robert sent him to me, to help heal my pain and for someone to love.

My two adventurers. For the 10 months they were together, they were inseparable.

Chapter 18

The End of a Career

Throughout Robert's last two months, and the three months after his death, I stayed in contact with my work colleagues and boss. The company I had worked for had been very generous, always supporting me, allowing me the leave I needed to be with Robert and work flexibly to be able to take Robert to his appointments.

Now that Robert had died, they were also supporting me with being able to take as long as I needed before heading back to work.

In August, two months after Robert's death, I caught up with my boss in Brisbane. We had dinner together and he wanted to know how I was holding up. What I had been doing and just making sure I had everything I needed at home. There was no talk of you need to come back, but rather when you do make the decision, we are happy to ease you back into work.

Over these few months I really could not have gone back to work. I led a large group of employees that ran construction teams, liaising with contractors, other executives in the company and dealing with customers. Many of the decisions we had to make to satisfy our customers were pretty straight forward, and I was starting to reflect on previous meetings, previous discussions and had to assess whether I wanted to continue to do this.

After the last five months, I had changed. My tolerance for people that whinged or stressed about things that really were not about life or death started to grate on me. I would get impatient and did not want to hear about it.

I also found that I had become very practised at making decisions quickly. Making the decisions that I had had to in the hospital about taking Robert to ICU, resuscitation and stopping treatment all had to be made quickly and rationally. At work, some decisions would take weeks, sometimes months and I did not know how I was going to cope with this.

I also had to decide on whether I wanted to go back to a desk job for the most part, and how was I going to fit travel in living up here by myself. Did I want to deal with employees and their problems? Did I have enough left in me to give to others, or was I spent. Was I at the point that I did not need others to depend on me, to depend on my knowledge, my advice, my care?

In September, after I returned from Vietnam, after losing my dogs and after thinking about myself for once, I made the decision to inform my boss that I would resign.

The day I told my boss, he was not surprised. He thought when we met in August that this might have been my decision and that he was also happy that I had thoroughly thought it through from a personal, financial, and business point of view. I told him that I was not the person that my people used to know and did not have the energy to give them or the business and that it would not be good for them or me to return.

Then came the day to make it official. I dialled into a meeting that had my peers and direct reports on. He gave them the news and gave me a wonderful wrap on all that I had achieved over the 25 years I had worked for this company. Some were shocked, others expected it and it gave me a chance to thank everyone for their support, their messages over the last five months and what had enabled me to come to this decision.

The company gave me one last dinner in October where I just invited an intimate team. I did not want the big fanfare. I was not leaving because I was off to some new job. I was leaving because I had changed, my life had changed, and it was time to find myself and a new purpose for the future.

I could not have been any more grateful for the managers and staff that had assisted, supported, and cared for me over the last six years. I walked away from an amazing caring company, with skills, knowledge, and achievements that I would have never thought was possible 25 years ago.

But more importantly, I walk away with pride in knowing that I did this my way and with several amazing friendships that I will have for the rest of my life.

Chapter 19

A Year of Firsts

Starting to sift through the paperwork, the accounts that needed to be closed and going over the same story again and again was one of the first tasks that I needed to undertake. The calls that started with "Hello my name is Suzanne Gomes, my husband Robert Gomes died on the 10th of June and I need to close his account, his membership.". It took me weeks and months to be able to change accounts into my name and engage a solicitor to start the probate process.

One of the hardest tasks came in April, during the COVID-19 isolation, cleaning out Robert's wardrobe. I had procrastinated for 10 months since Robert had died and decided during this period that it needed to be done.

Over the first 20 minutes I cried. The items that brought back memories of wonderful times and how sexy my husband looked in them. The smell of him still on those clothes made me hug some of them and I did not want to let go. But I also knew that I could not keep these items, they needed to go to a new home and in a lot of cases to his family and friends.

There were so many pieces that Robert had not worn. There were clothes with tags on them, there were pieces that had only been worn once or twice. Then there were all Robert's jackets and suits.

Robert was a bit of a fashionista and bought good quality clothes. He loved looking good and wore his clothes well. There was nothing better than going to a formal function and seeing Robert in a suit. He had this aura and attractiveness that made me proud to stand by him.

Then as the hours went by, I started to curse him. Why do you have so many clothes, so many shoes, so much of everything, I thought. Although more than half had been bought by me, and I am sure that was what Robert would have been saying from above. After four hours of sorting through everything, bagging up clothes for his brother, my brother, his mates, my friends adult kids and my nephews, the wardrobe was clean with only a few sporting jumpers and jackets that I could wear.

It was an emotional four hours with a little bit of joy thrown in. I had never wanted to see that wardrobe half empty; another part of Robert gone. But the reality was I had to do it and I was grateful that I had been able to give a small piece of Robert to the men in his life that will be proud to wear them.

In August, two months after Robert died, I undertook a 55-kilometre walk over two days through the Sunshine Coast Hinterland to raise money for the Leukaemia Foundation. The Foundation were there for us throughout Robert's illness and they provide so many services that several leukaemia friends have accessed. They also undertake vital research to find a cure, so I wanted to help their cause and be part of a team that included my Unplugged Teammates.

Our team of six was called 'Unplugged – Hike for Rob', made up of Heinke, Richard, Tom, Bruce, Tina and myself. We had all completed several hikes together or with others. We were fit, but it was the mental strength that I needed to get through these days. On several occasions when the hills were steep or my feet were aching, I reached out to Robert to get me through. I would never give up or not complete such an important event, but I needed his fight, his strength, a sign, to know that he was there watching us and getting us through.

At the end of the hike, I cried. I cried because we had made it, I cried because I have such wonderful friends that completed this with me, I cried because I realised the strength, courage and determination that I was continuing to build as a result of Robert's influence was inside of me.

As a group, we raised more than $10,000 for the Leukaemia Foundation. A great feat and, most of all, it was all raised in the memory of my gorgeous husband, Robert!

Two days after the hike, I ventured over to Vietnam for 10 days to meet up with my friends, John and Di. It was a great opportunity to take some time out and spoil myself while I still had my parents in Queensland.

The flight over was great. It certainly was different going overseas by myself, without Robert in the seat next to me, or even just travelling for leisure instead of work this time. When we were coming into land at Changi Airport in Singapore, the song over the PA system caught me by surprise. It was the instrumental version of 'Rainbow Connection', the last song played at Robert's funeral. Another sign or a beautiful moment where I could feel his warmth.

I started to sing along, and tears flowed down my face. I was incredibly grateful to be sitting by myself so that no one could see my tears.

Over the 20-plus years that I have known John and Di, Robert and I had enjoyed many trips away with them. From our first trip to Bali in 2000, and then nearly every two to three years after that. To the many weekends away at their houseboat, to their milestone birthdays on short cruises, to our last trip together in Broome in 2017. We have so many shared memories, fun times and lots of hangovers. Our love for travelling has allowed us to have many trips together, and now, travelling by myself, that I could do the first one with them.

Over the 10 days, we dined at some amazing restaurants, frequented many bars, had a mini two-night stay in Hoi Ann, and met some wonderful people who became friends.

One afternoon when Di and I went for a massage, I had a spiritual experience. Over the years since injuring my shoulder on the hike in Tasmania in 2017 I have been having massages every fortnight. They help with removing the stress in my body during my physical and mental challenges, and I enjoy the hour of thinking of nothing but being pain-free.

We sat at the end of the massage table, inhaling the soothing aroma of lemongrass and lavender, while the ladies massaged our feet and legs. Afterwards, in a state of bliss, we laid down on our backs as the masseuses started to knead our shoulders, releasing weeks of stress and tension.

As I turned over, I had a vision. With my eyes closed but still awake, I saw Robert standing on the beach, waving me over, gesturing for me to follow him. I had seen him in this place before. It was in 2011 when we went to Bali. He was wearing the same clothes in the pictures I had taken when we were walking on the beach.

I opened my eyes, looked left, and made sure Di was still there. She had her eyes closed enjoying her massage, so I shut my eyes and Robert appeared again behind my closed lids, still gesturing to me to follow. Again, I opened my eyes and glanced at Di, before shutting them once more. Then I told him, talking to him in my head, that I could not come with him as I could not leave Di. He turned his back to me and started to walk away. In that split second, I checked on Di, realised I was not actually physically leaving her and decided to follow him in my vision.

As we walked along the beach, he disappeared, and he gave me a vision of the cabins we were to build together. He showed me the pictures of waterfalls that would hang on the wall behind the beds, something I could not picture up until now. He showed me the colours, decors of the bathroom and what the kitchenette would look like. It was all there in front of me.

He then showed me a vision of myself. I was in our shed and he was showing me using the drop saw, cutting used wood and making furniture out of it. I could not believe what I was seeing and that this was happening to me. I have never had visions where I was still consciously awake, only visions via dreams.

Then it was all over. I opened and shut my eyes, hoping he would return, but he had disappeared. The massage was nearly finished, and my vision had vanished, but left an imprint in my memory.

After the massage, I sat outside with Di, enjoying a cup of herbal tea and started to recount my vision to her. She was blown away, but also recognised that maybe this was why I came to Vietnam. To be able to open your mind and be relaxed enough for Robert to send me his thoughts, his visions.

Massages tend to leave me lightheaded and in need of rest, but this one was different. My head was asking so many questions yet was simultaneously thankful for what I had experienced.

When I returned home, I was so eager to find our Bali photos from 2011 to see if what I had seen was that. Sure enough, there was not only a photo of Robert standing on the beach in the same singlet, shorts, hat and sunglasses, but also a photo of him walking in front of me which I had taken as I followed several paces behind him. The pictures took my breath away and I still could not believe what I had experienced in Vietnam.

The trip to Vietnam had been one of friendship, love, calm, spirituality, and the realisation that I was now a single woman who could create wonderful memories with beautiful friends.

On returning home from Vietnam, my parents only had another five days with me. They had been in Queensland for basically six months and needed to return to Melbourne for several health check-ups.

What I may not have told you, is that my dad was turning 79 that year, and my mum 73. So, they were not spring chickens anymore. I was always worried during this time that Robert's death would take a toll on their health. They loved him like a son, even worshipped him and everything he said and did. Robert could do no wrong in their eyes, and my brother and I would always tease them about that. Sometimes, I thought they loved Robert more than me, and so I worried that his death would be hard for them.

I do believe they did do some healing at my place. My mum was such a strong woman that would never let her emotions affect me. My dad was a big softy at heart and although his heart was breaking, he made sure he was busy, completing the jobs Robert and him had talked about, serving a purpose that would make his son-in-law proud.

Again, I had a sad day where I would drop another two people at the airport terminal who I loved so much and have to say goodbye. The trip to the airport was noticeably quiet. Mum fell asleep and dad listened to the radio with me. We made a couple of comments about the talk-back segment, but that was it.

We all jumped out of the car, took the luggage out and then started to hug, say our goodbyes, and let the tears roll down our faces. I was so sad to see them go. But they had to go home, not only to their appointments but to my brother, sister in law, step grandson and their granddaughter. Four family members that were also dealing with the loss of their brother in law and uncle, and for my brother one of his best mates. So, after tight hugs and words of "I love you", they watched me drive away with a wave, as I waved back to them through my window.

Over this time, I felt that my love and affection for my parents had stepped up several notches. I never thought I could spend so much time with them and be so grateful for their unconditional love. To know that they could devote this much time to me, my healing to my health, I could not thank them enough for all that they had done. This time was never going to be lost on me and I felt I had a connection with them that I had never had before.

As I drove off, I started to cry. I missed them already and there also came the realisation that I was now officially starting my life by myself. It was just me and my dogs and no one else, the first time in my life.

Every September, we always caught up with the girls from work to celebrate several birthdays. It was a great night with our Brisbane mates that we never missed.

But in September 2019 it was different. It was a girls' lunch, no guys allowed, which may have or have not reflected Robert's passing.

I came down to Brisbane and stayed the night in a hotel on the river. I hadn't seen these girls since Robert's wake and I was ready to let my hair down.

As night fell, we were still drinking copious amounts of bubbles and one of the girls announced that, "Today is different, someone is missing". At first, I didn't know what she meant until they charged their glasses to Robert. Yes, Robert was missing, and this was the first day out that I had celebrating without him. I suddenly felt sick and started to cry with everyone else, but my instant reaction was to buy another bottle!

Bad choice that was, because after many more cocktails, shots and bubbles, I was very drunk. I loved these girls but at around 11 p.m.,

10 hours since the party started, I secretly snuck out of the bar and staggered back to my hotel.

I don't know how I didn't get run over that night, much less get back to my hotel and up to my room. But as I approached my room and opened the door, the feeling of sickness rose into my mouth and I rushed to the toilet. All that alcohol had been too much, and I became violently ill.

When I woke in the morning, I had the hangover from hell and then had to tackle the two-hour drive home. As I was driving, I started to have an anxiety attack. I rang my parents to distract me, but it wasn't enough. By the time I got to Nambour I was hyper ventilating and was having some terrible thoughts. Again, I pulled over and rang Meagan. I told her I wasn't feeling well and needed her help to calm myself down.

Still, after 20 minutes, nothing was working, I decided to hang up on Meagan, lie to her that I was ok, then take myself to the emergency department at the Nambour Hospital. I asked to see a counsellor as I was having an anxiety attack and I was thinking of driving off the road, possibly killing myself.

Thankfully, a counsellor came quickly and talked me through the episode. They gave me some collateral to read and asked me to ring someone and continue talking.

I still can't believe that I contemplated ending my life. I just wasn't coping after losing my husband, and then my dogs, and being alone. But I still had a rational mind to know that in some part I wanted to live.

I have never had those feelings since, now 12 months on from that episode. I sort further counselling, increased the dosage of my anti-depressants and feel that I am in a much better place now.

Grief affects people in so many ways and this event scared me. Since that day I have been very careful not to use alcohol as a way of getting through the bad days.

My first visit to Melbourne to visit Robert's grave was in October. I hadn't organised Robert's headstone yet which I also needed to do on this visit. Sitting down by Robert's grave gave me an ill feeling. It did not feel like Robert was in a casket beneath me, but I knew he was. I sat their talking out loud, hoping that he would hear me. When I started to tell him that I missed him, that I was doing ok, but I really wished I did not have to visit him here so early in my life, the tears rolled down my face. My throat started to choke up, the pain in my heart started and I just could not believe my husband was in the ground.

I did not have a lot to say on that day because I had made my own memorial at home, with a seat and would talk to Robert most days from there. I told him this and felt that he was with me in Queensland when I needed to talk to him, and this did not feel like the place I needed to mourn him.

I laid his favourite flowers, orange gerberas, at his grave and just sat there alone, crying.

I knew it was time to leave when the workers arrived to erect a headstone opposite Robert's grave. I said to Robert that he probably organised the timing so that I would not spend too long here. I knew this was not true, but Robert would think that himself. He would not expect me to spend lots of time here and that the visits did not have to be frequent.

A Year of Firsts

On the 27th of November, I was in Melbourne and had organised a get together with family and close friends. It would have been our twentieth wedding anniversary and if Robert had of been alive, I was planning to renew our vows.

Earlier that day, I had visited Robert's grave. This time it did not feel as awkward as the first. I laid the same flowers on his grave, the same kind that had been in our wedding bouquets. I talked to him about our wedding - the parts I loved, the tears that flowed on that day, and how happy I was being his wife.

Tonight, there were no speeches or dancing, there was just a group of people who loved Robert and I, that came together to support me. It was great seeing the extended family, including my nieces, nephews and god daughters. They all loved their uncle so much and wanted to be here supporting me.

When it came to thinking about organising what to do at Christmas, New Year's, and my birthday in February, it just seemed hard. I did not want to make a fuss of these occasions, but after talking to a counsellor and then reading a couple of books on grief, I knew I had to do something. Because being at home by myself was not the answer.

At Christmas, I decided to stay home and go to Kyran and Mitch's, who I had lived with before Robert died. They had invited me down there to have Christmas with their families and be surrounded with gorgeous caring people that would embrace me with love.

It was a beautiful day and I had gifted myself a necklace that I believed was from Robert. A few months earlier when I was working through all the documentation after Robert's death, I found a pendant in our safe. It was the letter 'S' with a couple of diamonds in it, something I had never seen before. Now, I had to believe Robert had bought it for me as I knew that no one else had given it to me and I had never seen the necklace before.

So, on Christmas Day, I put it around my neck, feeling Robert's presence with me. He had left this special gift for me to find and wear with pride.

That night I then went to Heinke and Richard's and had Christmas dinner with them and a few of their friends. It was so nice to be surrounded by these beautiful people and it enabled all of us to be there for each other when usually Robert would have been there too.

I again spent New Year's with the Kyran and Mitch at their caravan site in Coolum. It was a lovely gesture for me to spend this first New Year's Eve without Robert with these beautiful friends. I did not really want to celebrate the coming of the new year as it would be the first full year that I would be living by myself and I did not want to think about how I was going to do that.

I still cannot believe this, but about five minutes before midnight, which I was not aware of, Archie my new puppy, who I had taken with me, needed to go to the toilet. As the clock struck midnight, I was wandering around the caravan park with my new best mate, as if I were avoiding celebrating the coming of the New Year. It was like Archie, who I think of as my spirit dog, planned it, and when I arrived back at the campsite and said "Happy New Year" to my gorgeous friends, I was relieved that I had been able to talk to Robert by myself when the clock struck midnight.

For my birthday, I organised to go to the Gold Coast with John, Di, Richard, Heinke, Kyran and Mitch, and my mum and dad came up from Melbourne. We hired a house at Palm Beach and had lots of fun and created amazing memories together which again helped me get through these firsts.

It was also wonderful that my brother had a work conference on the Gold Coast two days later and the four us went out to dinner to celebrate my birthday with him.

All of these events were extremely painful for me, but I knew I had to be surrounded by my closest and dearest to be able to get through them. My friends knew how to care and show their love to me during these times and get me through the day without falling into some sort of deep grief.

I just had to make sure, knowing that Robert would not want me to be sad on these days, to enjoy the time with people that wanted to spend it with me, which would start to create new memories as a widow.

Mother's Day 2020 fell on the 10th of May, 11 months since Robert took his last breath. In the early hours of the morning when I awoke on Mothers Days, I did not expect to experience the emotions that I did.

I am not a mother, so Mother's Day has always been about celebrating with my mum, and Robert and I would joke about me being a mum to our 'fur baby'! It was never about me on these days, rather it was mainly about my mum and all she had done for our family and us over the last six years.

Today, I would ring Robert's mum on her first Mother's Day without her son. Even before I dialled those numbers, the tears started to roll. What was this emotion all about for me? It took me around 30 minutes before I could muster the courage to dial her number.

Thankfully by that time the tears had dried up and Robert's mum was overwhelmed with happiness that I had called her. She was so grateful and commented that I had made her day. This did cause a few tears between the both of us, but they quickly dried up and we had a lovely conversation.

When it came to calling my mum, there were no tears, and she was just so happy to hear my voice. We chatted for over an hour and at the end she commented that she knew today would be hard for me because of what it represented, 11 months since Robert had died.

My emotions heightened as the day wore on. Not as a mother, but a wife, and seeing my friends and family celebrate with their loved ones, while mine could not be by my side, caused hurt and pain to build up inside of me.

By the evening, I started to understand that my grief was far deeper than this one day. I started to realise all the countless days stretching out ahead of me that I wouldn't get to celebrate anymore.

No Mother's Day, no wedding anniversary, no husband's birthday or 'second birthday', no Father's Day, and no reason to celebrate Christmas, Easter or Valentine's Day if Robert couldn't be there to celebrate with me.

I hoped my perspective would change over time, but at that time, and even now, the days that always brought me joy now bring only sadness, pain, and tears. They are anniversaries and memories of a life once lived. They are deep in the past, but within the first year of losing Robert they are nothing to me.

I must admit I did have some friends and family sending me messages saying I hope Archie (my dog) is good today and hope he gives you lots of love. I know these were sent in good spirit but seriously not now, not today. Today they mean nothing and if anything, a reminder of everything I have lost.

Sitting on the hill at the back of my property, I sobbed for hours on end. I yelled at Robert, at myself, at my friends - I just yelled. The pain was from a place I had not seen since the day Robert died and all I knew to do was just let it out. Let it flow from every bone in my body until I could not cry or grieve anymore.

My life at this point needs rebuilding more than I ever imagined. I have baggage that I would not want to put on anyone. I still have anger, that I have lost a wonderful life and must build a new one alone from the rubble of my past one. I have lost my purpose in life, my confidence, determination, and some days, myself entirely.

The unexpected loneliness that creeps in is confronting. It takes my breath away, it hurts my heart, my head, and stings my eyes. It grabs me with full force and it creates the most awful thoughts in my head of why am I still here, what do I have to live for, how long do I continue to go through these sad, sad days.

My only motivation to go on is Robert. He would never want me to wallow. He would never want me to be this sad. He would say, "Get up off the ground, shake your sadness off and try again." Again, and again, and that is what I will continue to do for the rest of my life.

Over the last seven years, I have marked new anniversaries on the calendar: the 13th of September, the day Robert was diagnosed with leukaemia, and the 28th of November, the day of Robert's bone marrow transplant. Now, I had another anniversary: the 10th of June, the date of Robert's death. Before that day, I had thought about this date many times. What would it be like, how would I remember it, celebrate it, and what was the right term for this so-called anniversary?

During the 2020 COVID-19 isolation period, I was not able to travel to Robert's gravesite so it would have to be a day spent at home.

What I also did not realise is that during the four weeks leading up to his anniversary, I would remember, quite vividly what was happening on every day in 2019. I went back over the events of the day, the ones that made me smile, which there were not too many. But mostly the ones that made me sad. The days I had to make those horrendous calls, the days I spent holding Robert's hand and the days I would play tug a war with him because he did not want to concede.

The words and thoughts that occurred on that day were many. My frustration with Robert, my sadness, the amount of energy both physically and mentally that I had to put in to help him live another day. The loss I felt, the loneliness, the physical pain in my heart. The regret of things I did not do with Robert when he asked and the compassion. The pure exhaustion of a year that went too fast and all that I had achieved without my soul mate by my side.

On this day, two beautiful things happened. My parents, brother and sister in law visited Roberts grave and rang me. They put the phone next in front of Robert's grave. They laid the flowers I would've taken there and allowed me to have 10 minutes with my husband alone. It was such a thoughtful gesture, and I was grateful for my brother having done that for me.

The other thing that that made my day was the seven friends that made their way to my home to celebrate Robert's life. We had a small ceremony around Robert's memorial, and all poured some of our drinks into the garden as a toast to Robert. The beautiful gifts I received that memorialise Robert and the love that they showed me was more than I could've expected.

After consuming Robert's favourite meal, drinking his favourite alcoholic drinks, and playing his music, we all shared the best of the best stories about Robert. We laughed, we sang, and we celebrated Robert's life in the only way we knew how. The way Robert lived his life, with love, laughter and good times.

I don't expect the anniversary of Robert's death to get any easier. My heart will always break at the thought of losing him, and I will forever miss the love of my life.

I received this from Heinke and Richard and is the centre piece of Robert's memorial garden at home.

Over the last year, the little things have also hit me. The day I went grocery shopping for the first time and it cost half of what it used to. The aisles and shelves that I did not have to stop at anymore because I did not have to buy those items. The day I arrived at my girls' weekend and went to ring Robert to say I had arrived. The first invite that only had my name on it. All these events, plus so much more would tug at my heart and bring a level of sadness that this was now my new life.

Sixteen months on, sometimes I encounter a new 'first' and an emotion I did not expect to feel. I know that this will continue for many years to come, maybe even for the rest of my life. I know that celebrations like weddings, christenings, birthdays and all of those other events that I would normally attend with Robert will feel empty to some extent. But I remain an optimist, and although I may continue to feel pain, I also know that Robert will be there with me in spirit giving me the courage to celebrate in the way we always did.

Chapter 20

Moving Forward

Since the first anniversary of Robert's death, life has started to feel a little less empty and I have started to move forward.

Several questions that I had for myself are now being answered, and I believe the universe has listened to my intentions. I have started to do a lot of work on myself, eating better, drinking less and I have a purpose that I am going to accomplish.

Robert's and my dream of owning an accommodation business in our beautiful hideaway, will be realised and it will be called Coolabine Retreat. I am in the middle of designing and gaining approval for three cabins on my property and hoping to start building in 2021.

The three cabins will be named after birds that are seen in the valley. The romantic cabin will be called the 'Wagtail' as it now has significance in my life.

Not only do I see the Wagtail birds every time I am in the paddock where this cabin will be built, but it is also the name of the lawn where Robert is buried. If you are curious look up the meaning of the Wagtail. In some cultures, especially the indigenous, it is known as the spirit bird. The bird that comes to visit that has the soul of the spirit. Robert visits me every day in the form of this special bird, and that is why the wagtail is on the cover of this book.

The retreat will not only cater to families, couples and will accommodate pets, but I intend to run widow and widower retreats for those who, like me, have lost their own loved ones. It will be a time where we can come together, with likeminded people to understand that what we are feeling is normal after losing a partner.

To continue with my mindfulness, I regularly attend yoga classes and have started life drawing. Both hobbies, as well as other crafts, calm the mind and feed the soul. I practice guided meditation, deep breathing and finding stillness, to proactively cleanse the mind and renew my physical body.

Archie, my dog, is my soulmate and where I go, he goes. He is such a calm, loving soul. I know that Robert delivered him to me and whenever I feel lonely, I give him a big hug and the feeling disappears.

I have always wanted a horse, one of my childhood dreams, and in November 2019 I began to take horse riding lessons. In August 2020, I was fortunate to lease two horses. In the last four months of having them at home, Chant and Minty have brought me calm, healing and happiness. Animals are the best medicine, and these two beauties, with Archie, will continue to do that for me.

Unfortunately, due to the events of COVID-19 in 2020, I have not been able to travel which is a passion of mine. I had one trip to Melbourne before lockdown occurred in Queensland and unfortunately had to postpone an amazing trip to Patagonia in South America. I do not know if or when I will be able to take that trip, but I am sure it will occur one day when the borders open up and travel becomes possible once more.

I have decided to publish this book. After researching different companies, I found the perfect company, the Ultimate 48 Hour Author, to publish my story. The process I am undertaking with them is enabling me to heal, and once the book is available it will help others dealing with being a carer, the grief of losing a loved one, and continuing on with life in the aftermath.

I have also committed to writing a second book titled *From Corporate to Country*. A reflection of my 25 years living and working in the city and in corporate Australia and then living and working in the country. This book will have similarities of building a career in a male dominated industry and starting a small business in the country by myself on 35 acres. I can't wait to start writing this book and continue to share my story of resilience through adversity.

Then the question that some people are starting to ask: will there be someone else in my life? I am sure that, at some point, someone will enter my life, that will celebrate the new days with me and I know Robert wouldn't want me to spend my days alone. I do want someone who will spoil me, and I will spoil them. I do want to love again, to want to feel the embrace of someone who will protect me and laugh with me. When that time comes I will embrace it.

Robert will always be in my heart; be a part of me; I am the woman I am today because of Robert.

Robert was, and always will be, the love of my life.

I will love you till eternity.

About The Author

Suzanne was born in 1973 to Noel and Pat and grew up in the Western Suburbs of Melbourne with her brother, Paul. Always a good student, Suzanne loved dancing and reading.

After studying nursing at university, Suzanne instead found herself navigating a corporate career from a call centre consultant to a successful executive.

In 1997, Suzanne met Robert and they married in 1999. They lived in Hoppers Crossing in Melbourne, had a wonderful group of friends, and travelled to inspiring destinations around the world. Moving to Brisbane in 2009 to advance Suzanne's corporate career, they bought a house, continued to travel, and lived the laid-back Queensland lifestyle.

After Robert received the heartbreaking news of a leukaemia diagnosis in 2013 and battled his way through more than 50 rounds of chemotherapy, a bone marrow transplant and three relapses, he eventually lost his brave fight and passed away in June 2019.

Suzanne now lives by herself on 35 acres with the companionship of her dog, horses and chickens, and her wonderful friends and family. She has started to adapt to life on her own and hopes to inspire others with her story of love, loss and healing.

Acknowledgements

Writing this book over the last four years has been a rollercoaster of emotions. At times, I was able to write for hours; other times, I didn't want to write so much as a word. My motivation for telling my story is for widows, widowers and anyone who has lost someone they love to blood cancer to resonate with what I am going through, and feel their stories and struggles are acknowledged.

There are so many people that I want to thank: family, friends, workmates, and even strangers, that stood by both of us and helped us through the pain but gave us happiness too. I want them to know again how much I appreciate their love and support.

To my parents, you stood by Robert and I every step of the way. Your love, care, and selfless, uncomplaining dedication by putting your own lives on hold to support mine. I will be forever grateful. As soon as you knew I was writing about my journey, you encouraged me to finish and publish it. I know you are proud of me, for the woman I am, for the way I have survived, and I am so proud to be your daughter.

To my brother, Paul, you have done some incredible things to support Robert and I. You flew to Brisbane, even though you hate flying, just to be there for us. You organised the working bee at Coolabine. You always picked up the phone when I needed to chat, and you loved Robert like a brother. Family means so much to me, and if you ever need me, I will be there.

To my in-laws, I wish I could take your pain away every day of the year. No parent should have to bury their son, and I know the toll this has taken, and continues to take, on you. You have supported me and have been so loving, and I want you to know that you will always be my family.

Meagan and Shane, John and Di, Kyran and Mitch, Heinke and Richard - where do I start? You have been such beautiful, loyal, and loving friends. You continue to support me, through my grief, my happiness, and new adventures. I couldn't have given Robert the support and care he needed without you. We will be friends forever. I love you all.

To Meagan, Colleen and Denise, my 'Alphas'. Even when you were so far away, you were always with me. You gave me love and care from afar that I always felt you were right by my side. Our chats, our tears, your unwavering support, have been exactly what this girl needed. I love you all to the moon and back. Alpha strength together!

To all the family, friends and mentors who have known that I was writing this book, thank you. Thank you for encouraging me to finish it. Thank you for pushing me publish it. Thank you for buying my book before I printed it. You are my tribe, my people. I will be forever grateful for you supporting my new ventures.

Although I haven't named them, I can't thank the doctors, physicians, the nurses, the counsellors and all of the medical staff I have met over

Acknowledgements

the last seven years. Especially Robert's doctor who gave Robert six additional years that we didn't think were possible. All of you were our rock through the hard times and brought laughter through the good times. I will never forget your love and support. I am forever grateful.

Lastly, to the Ultimate 48 Hour Author team, Natasa, Stu, Lendy, Viv, Julie and Nik. From the first online workshop that I attended, I knew you were the team for me. I have loved working with you all. Your knowledge, enthusiasm, and drive have been just what I needed, not only for this book but for my life as a whole. The community you have brought together and the way you motivate us to stay on track is why your business is so successful. I look forward to working with you again in the future. Thank you!

Suzanne Gomes

Suzanne Gomes, before becoming a small business owner, was a corporate Executive in one of Australia's iconic companies. She led various large teams over 25 years and has spoken and chaired several major events.

Suzanne's life was turned upside down when her husband Robert was diagnosed with Leukaemia. Over the last six years, Suzanne's journal of Robert's treatment and the diary of her heartache, has now been turned into her first novel "From Wife to Widow".

Suzanne has spoken to groups about her struggles and her role as Robert's carer. Her story is about dealing with loss and grief, but also of love. Her insights are brave and inspirational and give the audience a raw insight to the reality of dealing with blood cancer.

She has enjoyed the journey of bringing this book to a reality. She has the drive to complete another book and continue to support widows and widowers.

Suzanne is available to speak to support groups and organisations on:

Being a carer
- Balancing work and life
- Having the right support systems in place
- Managing Anxiety

Dealing with Loss & Grief
- Sharing her experiences
- Expressing your emotions brings strength
- Where to get help

Life as a Widow
- What changes and how to deal with it
- How to make successful life changes
- Dreams for the future

Contact Suzanne:
- www.suzannegomes.com.au
- suzannegomes73@hotmail.com

www.ingramcontent.com/pod-product-compliance
Lightning Source LLC
Chambersburg PA
CBHW021434080526
44588CB00009B/520